Preface

This monograph presents the findings of a country case-study carried out within the Population Division's programme on 'Studies on the Status of Women in relation to Development and Demographic Behaviour'. Research on the status of women has broadened its perspectives to include an exploration of the differential effects of social and economic development upon the condition of women. The principal aim of this research programme is to identify relationships between socio-economic development and demographic trends and to analyse their impact on women's role within the family, their participation in the labour force and migration and fertility patterns. There are evidently enormous national as well as regional differences in women's position in the family and in their social and economic status, and these studies are designed to elucidate the precise nature of those differences and their implications for women and development in the countries concerned.

The present study, implemented by Graciela Taglioretti, provides an interesting example of the complex interrelationship between women's involvement in the labour market, migratory processes and socio-economic development. The author analyses the evolution of women's participation and level of insertion in the labour force with reference to internal as well as external migratory processes using the census data for 1963 and 1975. These findings are then related to overall cultural and socio-economic factors and integrated within a comparative framework. The results indicate a significant correlation between international migration and a substantial increase in female participation in the labour force, particularly in the middle sectors of the economy, implying that women operate as a replacement labour force and only achieve mobility under such conditions.

The relatively greater increase in married women working and the enhanced economic visibility of rural and urban women can both be seen as a direct response to economic pressure on family income.

This exploratory study should be of particular interest to policy-makers and those concerned with the effects of development upon female status since it confirms that economic stagnation and the subsequent drop in living standards give rise to two apparently interrelated phenomena: emigration and a marked increase in women's participation in the labour force at various levels. To ensure women's continued access to occupations in improved economic conditions would require the development of a supportive infrastructure and increased opportunities for acquiring competitive skills, thus creating a basis for women's true incorporation into the labour market.

The opinions expressed are those of the author and do not necessarily reflect the views of Unesco.

Women in a world perspective

Also in this series:

Women as heads of households in the Caribbean: family structure and feminine status, by Joycelin Massiah

Dynamics of the female labour force in Argentina, by Zulma Recchini de Lattes

Women and work in Uruguay

Graciela Taglioretti
Centro de Informaciones
y Estudios del Uruguay

Unesco

The designations employed and the presentation of material throughout this publication do not imply the expression of any opinion whatsoever on the part of Unesco concerning the legal status of any country, territory, city or area or of its authorities, or concerning the delimitation of its frontiers or boundaries.

Published in 1983 by the United Nations Educational,
Scientific and Cultural Organization,
7 place de Fontenoy, 75700 Paris
Typeset by Spottiswoode Ballantyne Ltd, Colchester (United Kingdom)
Printed by Imprimerie Floch, Mayenne (France)

ISBN 92-3-102110-9

Contents

1 Introduction

Between the years 1963 and 1975, two possibly interrelated phenomena could be observed in Uruguay: (a) an increase in women's participation in the labour market, in both rural and urban areas; (b) internal migratory processes of rural–urban and urban–metropolitan type, to which are added towards the second half of the period an atypical process of international emigration—estimates showing an approximate loss of 7.5 per cent of the original population. The interrelation between the two must be made explicit, in order to grasp the significance of the increasing participation of women in the labour market. The present work intends to explore the characteristics of both phenomena, so as to establish some hypotheses concerning developments in the socio-economic conditions of Uruguayan society.

In the first place, a brief description of the context is given in order to provide the principal macrostructural elements which make further analysis possible.

Secondly, international emigration and the main migratory movements by sex (rural–urban, interior (rest of the country)—Montevideo (metropolis)) are analysed.

Thirdly, the modality of women's increasing participation in the labour market is analysed, together with the way in which it is reflected in the internal composition of the labour force, focusing on three aspects: branch of activity, category of occupation and occupation.

Finally, by way of conclusion, some hypotheses put forward in the course of the analysis are summarized.

As far as the interrelationship between the two phenomena is concerned, the study is exploratory. There are no existing sources of information—except with reference to some characteristics of international emigration—which include both dimensions simultaneously. It is not therefore possible to go beyond the level of hypothesis about the problems to be studied.

Some conceptual and empirical clarification of the levels of disaggregation used should be given here.

Three areas are proposed: rural interior, urban interior and Montevideo (metropolis). With regard to the labour market, this trichotomy does not mean the existence of three independent labour markets, but rather that they are seen as a unit of parts which may be analysed separately, in terms of some specific characteristics.[1] The internal distinction in the labour market is based on two combined criteria: a sectoral one—preponderance of the primary sector in the rural area—and a demographic one—degree of labour force concentration in the urban area. This makes it possible to differentiate between the Montevidean labour market, with a high concentration of the secondary and tertiary sector, and that of the interior, characterized by its low concentration.

Strictly speaking, the labour market as a whole will not be analysed, but the emphasis will be placed on one of its components: the labour force supply. It should also be noted that the subdivisions do not imply that the areas are considered as totally homogeneous, but rather that they contain different situations. In relation to labour demand, the rural area, for example, has at least two clearly differentiated situations: intensive production with intensive use of manpower and extensive production with low manpower use (Niedworok and Prates, 1979). At the urban level, it is possible to distinguish capital-intensive and labour-intensive activities (Fortuna, 1980). However, in spite of this diversity, the areas have predominant characteristics which make a unified analysis possible, bearing in mind that the analysis of the labour market is of interest in relation to migratory processes. The rural areas tend to expel their population and Montevideo remains receptive at the national scale. It is receptive but not attracting, for although the city responds to the arrival of the population from the interior, this does not reflect its capacity to absorb manpower. This situation remains constant and, for a general analysis of the migratory processes, the proposed disaggregation is reasonably adequate. At this level, the major difficulty is not conceptual, but empirical.

It is not possible to provide a complete picture of the migratory processes because of the limitations of available data. The information about internal migratory flows in the 1960–63 period gives a view of the trends between urban and rural areas in the interior of the country, as

1. Marshall (1978, p. 32) points out the unity of the labour market. 'One of the most manifest forms of the existence of a process of unification in the labour markets [particular] is constituted by the migration of labour force [internal and international].' The brackets are ours.

well as those directed towards Montevideo. The quality of the data makes it preferable to exclude from the analysis flows corresponding to movements of urban origin and rural destination, as well as those from Montevideo towards the interior.[1] However, the economic stagnation with the important consequence of international emigration in the 1963–75 period, and some regularities observed in other contexts, make it possible to establish as the most plausible hypothesis that in the Uruguayan case there occurs what has been called 'migration by stuffing.[2] The importance of the expulsion factors together with a situation of economic stagnation is of such dimensions that it seems hardly reasonable to assume that there are no relevant counter streams.[3] Their existence is not denied but priority is given to expulsion factors. This approach is based on the consideration of macrostructural elements.

Lastly, it should be pointed out that the migration analysis is not carried out in an isolated fashion, and that omissions in information can reasonably be remedied by a study of population movements within a wide spectre of demographic variables and in relation to the main macrostructural phenomena. With this information as a whole and from its internal consistency, it is possible to establish reasonably well-founded hypotheses. The approach of this study justifies it beyond its empirical limitations, taking into account the almost total lack of studies of women's participation in the labour market.

1. Data on urban–rural migration for 1963 are not trustworthy when incorporated into the wider context of demographic variables; net masculine balance is favourable for the rural area. As regards the data for the Montevideo–rest of the country area for the same year, it is frankly erroneous: it registers only fifty-one migrants.
2. McGreevey (1968) mentioned by Cardona and Simmons (1978).
3. In this respect Lee (1965, p. 294) states: 'The efficiency of the stream (ratio of stream to counter stream or the net redistribution of population effected by opposite flows) is high if the major factors in the development of a migration stream were minus factors at origin.'

2 The context

In order to understand these two phenomena of massive international emigration and massive incorporation of women into the labour market, one must take into account not only economic levels but also an aggregate of socio-cultural elements which operate as intermediating or secondary variables. The socio-cultural structure of a society is the result of prolonged processes over time and this justifies reverting—though briefly—to the first decades of this century.[1]

The period up to 1955

Uruguay has historically depended on foreign demand for its primary products.[2] Although this situation of dependency conditioned its whole economy, up to the mid-1950s the export of the surplus livestock production favoured a true economic expansion, accompanied by a process of social modernization. This can be traced to the first decades of the present century.

Uruguay is a highly urbanized country—in 1908 40 per cent of the population was to be found in urban areas, 30 per cent of them living in Montevideo. This characteristic is mainly due to two factors. There was

1. Nahum (1975, p. 3) states with regard to this period: 'The work carried out during the first third of this century has proved important and, in some sectors, irreversible. The value of political democracy, the pacific struggle of opposing parties, the extension of education, the role of the State as arbitrator in social conflicts were concepts which slowly were incorporated into the mentality of the Uruguayans and which gave them a definite and characteristic personality with respect to the rest of Latin America.'
2. During the periods 1906–10, 1930, 1950 and 1970, agricultural and cattle-breeding production accounted for 94.9, 93.3, 98.4 and 91.8 per cent respectively, of total exports (Macadar et al., 1971).

a general trend of rural to urban migration and in particular of female migration because of the predominating type of exploitation, which was extensive livestock breeding (Prates, 1976). There was also fairly large-scale immigration of persons of European origin.

This urbanization process was facilitated by modernizing projects in the urban industrial sectors which were carried out by the liberal-oriented party in power. Such projects were made possible by the transfer of a part of the surplus from the rural sector, which did however not imply a questioning of the economic power of the livestock sector.[1]

The policy of support for the urban sectors—conditioned by the existing structure of landholding and extensive cattle-breeding exploitation—consolidated the structure of the country: a large seaport-city (Montevideo) centralizing the necessary services for the agro-exporting sector and an extended urban network which, to a large extent, is a consequence of the high expulsive factor of the rural sector (Cocchi et al., 1977). The action of the state both directly and indirectly favours the creation of large urban middle sectors. This is a direct influence because of the numerous functions the state assumes which make it an important employer in medium-sized dependent sectors. It also occurs indirectly because of the backing the state gives to artisan industry—in 1908, 6,300 industrial establishments had an average of nine workers—thus contributing to the creation of independent sectors of small owners. This industrial growth favoured the participation of women in the labour market: the manufacturing industry shows the greatest development—especially in food and clothing—to which must be added 'the heavy demand of the rising industrial capitalism for a highly abundant and extremely cheap labour' (Barran and Nahum, 1979, p. 75). Thus women's participation is high and especially so when considered that, in contrast with the other countries of the area, it is a practically urban participation. In 1908 the refined rate of activity reached 18.0 per cent.

The support the urban sectors received from the state was accompanied by a policy of improvement of the population's standard of living: a massive development of education, the creation of health services, the promotion of civil and labour legislation which was very

---

1. Quijano (1972) in his analysis of the fiscal policy for the period arrives at the following conclusions: 'by all this we wish to prove the tributary measures imposed during the period 1900–1930 did not signify a confrontation with the cattle-breeding bourgeoisie. The increase in the percentage of the added value on agriculture directly appropriated by the State through taxes is very small at a time of important increase in the surplus in that sector and when the State apparatus was considerably expanded.' Furthermore, the property holding was not altered. Gini's index on the concentration of land property has values which corroborate this statement: 1918: 74.0; 1951: 81.8; 1961: 82.5; 1970: 82.5.

advanced for its time.[1] Within this context, women occupy an important place and are the object of concrete decisions which—apart from their protective character—favour women objectively. There is for example a law on divorce making the decision that of the wife. It was passed in 1913 and allowed her the possibility of becoming the head of the family, with all the accompanying connotations of independence *vis-à-vis* men. A law was passed in 1915 granting expectant mothers forty days' leave, while in 1918 the so-called 'law of the chair' was passed stipulating that working women should have chairs to sit on when their tasks permitted it.

A number of phenomena result from the efforts of the large middle sectors to compensate for the reduction in their income and the decrease in their standard of living. Some of these are multiple jobs, pensioners continuing to work with the resulting reduction of opportunities for the young to enter the labour market and the devaluation of education. It is worth while considering this last phenomenon because of the central role education plays in the process of modernization.

From the beginning of this century, education is not only influenced by an egalitarian policy but especially by a labour market which is constantly growing and diversifying and which requires specialized labour. During the crisis, education, which for decades had been legitimized as a channel for social upward mobility, acquired a dynamic of its own and its expansion continued: indeed its rhythm of growth accelerated independently of the change in the conditions in which it had originated. This was to be expected: education has a market value and to the extent that the general levels increase, it becomes necessary to surpass those levels to be in a position to compete 'and maintain one's market share' (Thurrow, 1972).

Thus between 1955 and 1975 the registration of pupils in primary education increased by 25 per cent, that for secondary education, because of its lower initial penetration, increased by 183 per cent and registration in university education by 117 per cent. These increases are reflected in a considerable improvement in the educational levels of the population and especially those of women. This may be seen in Figure 1.

In this manner, the ever-widening offer of education leads to its devaluation. An indicator in this respect is the reduction in the range between the maximum and minimum salaries of the technical-professional staff and service personnel of the central government: while

1. 1914: first law of compensation for discharged employees; 1915: the 8-hour working day law was passed, 48-hour working week, one day of rest for every seven days worked, the prohibition of work for minors of less than 13 years of age; reduced working day for minors of 16 years of age; 1919: old-age pensions law; 1930: civil responsibility of employers with regard to accidents at work and the workers' right to compensation (Gonzalez, 1976).

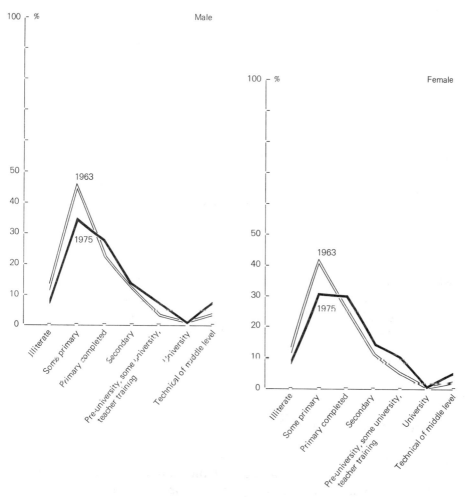

FIG. 1. Uruguay: educational levels of the population of 15 years and over, 1963 and 1975 (after National Censuses, 1963 (definitive data) and 1975 (preliminary sample)).

in 1961 the relation was of 2.2 for the maximum salaries and 2.5 for the minimum ones, in 1969 it stands at 1.7 and 1.4 respectively (Bilgueria, 1970).

All these mechanisms which the system developed to maintain the socio-political equilibrium were relatively useful during a short period, but towards 1965 what was objectively to constitute the last resource was initiated: a massive emigration of the population with the characteristics that will be studied.

In 1879 the law of common education established access to primary education for all children of both sexes between the ages of 5 and 15 (Rial, 1980), with the result that around 1908 the female literacy rate was practically the same as that of males. The creation in 1910 of the Feminine Section of Secondary Education increased the percentage of women students at that level from 0.5 per cent prior to 1916 to 7 per cent in 1916 (Barran and Nahum, 1979).

15

At the time of the 1929 crisis, the level of social development, the growing process of diversification and occupational ramification, and above all, the relatively important distribution of income, made a reduction in the standard of living and of consumption impossible without entailing important social and political consequences. The method chosen to confront this new situation was the process known as substitutive industrialization. In this way, two basic demands were met: on the one hand, the demand of the consumer society could be met and, on the other, the growth of activities already existing in the country was encouraged, thus generating employment. The substitutive process[1] was allowed to feed itself, which necessarily presupposes a scheme for the distribution of income and for increase in real salaries. The industry which developed was light industry and its aim was to satisfy internal demand. It depended on the import of industrial inputs and also of raw material. Exports were almost entirely of agricultural origin and did not increase during this period; imports followed the rhythm of industrial growth.

About 1955 and following on the unfavourable post-Second World War situation and the end of the Korean War, Uruguay's agricultural production deteriorated noticeably. In addition, the cost of industrialized products could not compete in foreign markets while the local market was very small.

Possibilities offered by the system for the development of industrialization were exhausted. From 1955 onwards, the economic growth of Uruguay, initiated at the beginning of the century, was interrupted.

Before moving to the following period, it is important to stress some aspects of legislation which, both directly and indirectly, favoured women. During this period women obtained several important benefits: at the political level, the law of equal civil rights was passed in 1932 and enforced in 1938, with the entry of the first woman as a member of parliament registered in 1943. In 1950 the compensations payable to expectant mothers in the event of their discharge from work, were established (Rial, 1980). The growth of industry and the accompanying union activities resulted in the establishment in 1943 of an authority for the regulation of salaries. That same year, benefiting the most important industrial trade union, the system of family allowances entered into operation, offering considerable social benefits, to both men and women workers and their children.

---

1. (Instituto de Economía, 1969) gives an excellent overall picture for the Uruguayan economic process. Many of the figures mentioned here appear there.

The period 1955–74

The regressive evolution of the per capita Gross National Product (GNP) illustrates the stagnation of this period: the index moves from 100 for the period 1951–55 to 89.7 for the period 1966–68. This situation occurs in an inflationary process, as a result of the struggle of the different social sectors to maintain their participation in the social product. The evolution of the consumer index is a good indicator in this respect: the rate of annual growth of the cost of living spiralled constantly from 9 per cent in 1955 to 135 per cent in 1968. As was to be expected, this was reflected in the distribution of income and directly affected the salaried sectors. This is evident in the decrease in real salary: if the average for 1961–63 be taken as 100, the index drops in the year 1975 to 74 for the public sector and to 67 for the private sector, the decline is constant starting from 1971.

At the same time in the 'passive' sectors (*pasivos*) which in 1969 represented 30 per cent of the total of active workers, pensions were reduced by 50 per cent over a period of 6 years: the average pension drops from 100 in 1963 to 50 in 1969.

The state, which plays a major role in all the Uruguayan process, from 1955 onwards increased the number of functions it had traditionally fulfilled: with occupational opportunities progressively closing down, it became an important employer. Between 1955 and 1969 the number of public employees increased by 28 per cent and what is more, the state absorbed 50 per cent of the jobs created during this period (Macadar et al., 1971). Thus, a long-standing phenomenon in Uruguay became still more acute: in 1908 the tertiary sector absorbed 45 per cent of the economically active population (EAP), 49 per cent in 1955 and 52 per cent in 1975.

It should be pointed out that from 1975 new policies have been successful in positively reversing some of the macro-economic tendencies mentioned (in particular the per capita production and the rate of investments), although at considerable social cost (the decrease in real salary and more so in the case of pensions). It must be added, however, that the information available suggests international emigration has decreased its rate and (household surveys for 1975–79 in Montevideo) that women's participation in the economically active population continues to increase.

3 Migratory processes

General demographic characteristics

It is useful to give first a general view of some demographic characteristics of Uruguayan society. Later, on the basis of the analysis of the migratory movements—particularly international emigration—many of the aspects emphasized will be seen to be the result of a particular contextual evolution. However, the characteristics in themselves are relevant because of the limits they set to the potential availability of manpower.

From Table 1 it can be seen that as regards distribution by age, Uruguay is very different from the rest of the countries in the region except for Argentina, which presents some differences. Uruguay has a noticeably aged pyramid of which the features become more acute towards 1975: the under-14 age-group is the proportion which decreases most, followed by the 15–64 age-group, the counterpart being that in 1975 almost 10 per cent of the poulation was over 65. This distribution on the whole reflects characteristics which have been shaping the pyramid from the first decades of this century and which are the result of the social development described earlier—low birth rates and high life expectancy at birth. It is also, however, the product of a migratory phenomenon.

As regards distribution by sex, the general tendency points to a reduction of the sex ratio, Montevideo showing the lowest percentage of males, followed by the other urban areas, while the rural areas show a high sex ratio, a feature which is common to most Latin American countries (Elton, 1978).

With reference to Table 1, two fundamental aspects should be pointed out about the spatial distribution of the population: one half lives in the capital of the country with over 80 per cent in the urban area.

18

TABLE 1(a). General demographic characteristics, 1963–1975

Characteristics	1963	1975
Total population (in thousands)	2 595.5	2 782.0
Distribution of population by regions (%)		
Montevideo (metropolis)	46.3	44.5
Interior (rest of the country)	54.7 (100)	55.5 (100)
Urban	(67.0)	(73.0)
Rural	(33.0)	(27.0)
Sex ratio by regions		
Total	98.9	96.1
Montevideo	91.2	87.8
Interior	106.0	103.3
Urban	95.7	94.3
Rural	130.6	132.8
Population structure by age-group (%)		
0–14	28.2	27.0
15–64	64.2	63.2
65 and over	7.6	9.8

Source: National Censuses, 1963 (definitive data), 1975 (preliminary sample). (Only three censuses have been undertaken in this century, in 1908, 1963 and 1975.)

TABLE 1(b). General demographic characteristics, 1963–75. Mean annual growth rate of population by sex and by region

Age-group/region	Male	Female	Total
Total population			
Montevideo	0.08	0.40	0.25
Interior	0.78	1.00	0.89
Urban	(1.55)	(1.68)	(1.62)
Rural	(−0.77)	(−0.91)	(−0.83)
TOTAL	0.47	0.72	0.60
Population aged 15–64			
Montevideo	−0.17	0.18	0.01
Interior	0.90	1.15	1.02
Urban	(1.68)	(1.82)	(1.74)
Rural	(−0.51)	(−0.72)	(−0.59)
TOTAL	0.42	0.67	0.55

Source: National Censuses, 1963 (definitive data), 1975 (preliminary sample). (Only three censuses have been undertaken in this century, in 1908, 1963 and 1975.)

As to the population growth, the annual mean growth rate (per cent) is remarkably low (0.6) and the male growth rate is lower than the female one. The growth of the potentially active population (15–65 years) is lower than that of the total population, the male growth rate being relatively lower than the female. Undoubtedly, the most important feature is the variation by large regions and by sex.

During the period, the growth rate of the population in Montevideo is far lower than that of the rest of the country, the potentially active population remaining the same as in 1963. Within the latter, the male growth rate decreases, whereas the female one increases very slowly.

In the rest of the country, on the other hand, the growth of the total population is higher, the female growth rate being more pronounced than that for males. Logically and because of the weight of the urban population on the total population, these characteristics appear in the urban area, though with higher values.

In contrast to this, the rural population shows a considerable decrease; that of the population as a whole being greater than that of the potentially active population. Undoubtedly, the most outstanding feature is the difference by sex: the female population decreases more than the male. This trend can be seen in the data from the agricultural censuses.

International emigration

The volume of international emigration makes it the factor with the greatest influence on demographic changes.

The analysis of this phenomenon is based on three sources of information: estimate figures of the General Directorate of Statistics and Censuses (Dirección General de Estadística y Censos, 1979), the Survey on International Emigration carried out by the Directorate (1976), and the Niedworok (1979a) estimated figures.

The first source gives an estimation of emigration obtained from population projections by sex and age between 1963 and 1975 for the whole country—from which immigration for the period will be subtracted.

The second source is the survey carried out in Montevideo in 1976. The information requested from the persons surveyed set no limits as regards origins. However, the fact that it was made among a representative sample of households in the department of Montevideo and that queries about emigration were limited to a given degree of kinship to the surveyed person, there was necessarily an under-representation of the emigrants going abroad from other parts of the country.

The third source gives estimated figures of international emigrants during the intercensal period, and in particular their distribution by year of departure, based on census data. It also incorporated elements of the

International Emigration Survey to estimate the relative weight by sex.

Although the figures obtained vary according to the sources, this information gives quite a good picture of the outstanding characteristics of emigration. None of the sources of information may be considered as complete in itself, but together they offer a larger aggregate of data, of which the internal consistency serves as a basis for hypothesis.

Estimates of the volume of emigration show an approximate figure of 7.5 per cent of the total population at the beginning of the intercensal period. As to the structure of emigration by sex and age, the sources differ: while estimates of the Directorate of Statistics show a distribution of 50 per cent for men and women, the Survey of International Emigration—and reasonably the estimate based thereon (Niedworok, 1979a)—gives 55 per cent for men and 45 per cent for women. These differences may be due to the greater relative weight of the Montevideo population in this survey. In fact, Montevideo shows a relative greater decrease in the sex ratio. However, given the decrease of the sex ratio for the country, it seems reasonable to suppose that migration has in fact been predominantly masculine.

All sources indicate that emigrants are mainly young persons. Estimates of the Directorate of Statistics show that 47 per cent of emigrants in 1975 were between the ages of 20 and 39, to which it must be added that distribution by sex in this age-group favours men: 46 per cent are women and 54 per cent men. As will be seen later, this differential distribution is a supplementary element for the interpretation of women's entry into the labour market.

While the preceding figures bear out the consequences of emigration in the age and sex distribution of the population at the end of the period, the survey data refer to the age of emigrants at the time of departure. This provides for a closer approximation to the emigrants' motives, especially if they are supplemented with data on the levels of occupation of the emigrants given in Table 2. As regards age at the time of departure, 76 per cent of the migrants were between 20 and 49 years of age, of which 55 per cent were men and 45 per cent women.

Distribution of emigration during the course of the period shows that 83 per cent of men and 82 per cent of women left the country between 1970 and 1975 and, within this period, of the total emigrants, 55.2 per cent were men and 44.8 per cent women (Niedworok, 1979a).

The focus is now on the most relevant variables which characterize emigration (Table 2). As the interest is centred in bringing to the fore the selectivity of emigration, the values given are those of the variables with percentages exceeding the parameters of the resident population. In this respect and because of the limitations about the representativeness of the survey, both the parameters for the total of the country as well as those for Montevideo are given.

TABLE 2. Selectivity of international migration

Variable	Value	Migrants			Total Uruguay (1975)			Total Montevideo		
		Male	Female	Total	Male	Female	Total	Male	Female	Total
Marital status[1]	Married	58.8	70.1		55.6	52.7		59.5	51.0	
Educational level[2]	Secondary			32.4			18.7			N.D.
Type[3] of activity[4]	EAP	87.3	51.2		77.1	28.9		71.3	31.8	
	unemployed and seek work first time (% of EAP)	24.1	13.0		6.7	6.8		6.4	7.0	
Occupation[5]	Craft workers and labourers			27.3			16.9			19.2
Branch of activity[5]	Manufacturing industry			34.4			19.1			24.9
Category of occupation[5]	Private employee			62.2			47.8			50.0

1. Data supplied by this survey are of migrants aged 14 and over; data from the census cover those aged 15 and over.
2. The survey and the census took into account persons aged 15 and over.
3. Data for Montevideo are for population aged 12 and over.
4. Definition of economic activity is the same, both for the survey and the census.
5. Data for the census cover population aged 12 and over; the survey covers those aged 14 and over.
Sources: Survey of International Migration (Dirección General de Estadística y Censos, 1976); National Census, 1975 (preliminary sample).

The figures presented should be regarded with care since emigrants have an over-representation of young persons. The presentation of the data does not permit a control by age at the level of the variables included. However, the importance of some of the differences makes it possible to advance some reasonable hypotheses.

Taking into account the context and given the high levels of unemployment, it is reasonable to suppose that they were the main cause for the massive emigration. At the same time, it is the married persons—with a noticeable over-representation of women compared with the parameters of the resident female population—who leave the country, in other words those with more immediate responsibility.

Some variables point to a more socio-economic characterization of the persons and, given the growing deterioration of the net salary, it is from the dependent sectors that there is more emigration. The fact that the emigrants come from the private labour market—those of the public labour market showing much lower parameters in comparison with the residents—reveals the differences between these two types of dependency. The hours of work of a government employee are, as a rule, relatively short with a high percentage of the posts requiring 30 hours' work per week. Private situations, in general, surpass the 40-hour work week. The laxity in the reaction of the government to both absences and non-compliance with working hours is traditional, but this is not the case in private employment. In other words, government employees have much greater possibilities of supplementing their salaries with other jobs than private employees. To this must be added the fact that the state does not dismiss personnel because of the inability to pay salaries, and for this reason there is much less unemployment in this sector.

A further indicator of the socio-economic level of emigrants is their occupation which corresponds to the lower middle sectors: craft workers and labourers. This is accompanied by a selectivity according to educational level, which is another important factor for the socio-economic profile of the individuals. Low educational levels are under-represented among the emigrants: while the national total for the population age 14 and over without schooling or with primary schooling reaches 70 per cent (8 and 62 per cent respectively), the percentage among emigrants 15 years and over is 47 per cent. The major differences in educational attainment are found at the secondary level (32 per cent for migrants against 18 per cent for non-migrants) followed by the university level (5 per cent of migrants and 3.5 per cent among non-migrants).

Bearing in mind what was said about the expansion dynamics of formal education in Uruguayan society, this more defined emigratory behaviour among those having higher schooling is to be expected. The formal middle-level education—humanistic, for this category does not

23

include technical schooling—or higher education, legitimizes aspirations to middle and high-level occupations and, more important still, the standard of living and consumption these occupations offer. Because of the devaluation of education, these aspirations cannot materialize. In the same way, growing credentialism offers better opportunities to those who have reached higher levels of schooling, to enter other occupational markets in constant expansion, where formal middle-level education and, especially higher education, are not so devalued, in countries such as Brazil, Mexico and Venezuela. In this respect, it should be added that Argentina absorbs more than 50 per cent of the emigrants of active age. Emigration to that country, which is concentrated mainly in Buenos Aires, is similar in its distribution regarding its more relevant variables, to the parameters of non-migrants in Uruguay.[1]

This brief description of emigration leads to some conclusions. The prolonged economic crisis, which causes high levels of unemployment, appears to be the fundamental cause of emigration. Unemployment is concentrated among the young and mainly among young men. As regards the socio-economic level, although occupations falling within those of the lower middle sectors are over-represented, the educational levels of the emigrants are clearly higher than the national parameters, which are already considerably high by Latin American standards.

All this indicates that the economic situation influences, both directly and indirectly, the massive influx of women on to the labour market: directly, in that it encourages them to undertake remunerated work to compensate for the growing decrease in real salary, and indirectly, because through emigration, it liberates occupational positions thus granting women greater possibilities of access.

Internal migrations

Although the main limitations in sources for the study of internal migration have already been shown, further precision is necessary.

Only the 1963 census allows for an analysis of all the defined areas. The various migrations by sex and by size of city of destination are known. As regards age, only data by urban or rural area for migrants from the interior to Montevideo are available.

From the 1975 census it is possible to analyse interdepartmental migrations.[2] For the present study, only the analysis of migration from

1. Characteristics of migrations from Uruguay to Argentina are different from the other migrations to that country (Foucher, 1977).
2. The Department is an administrative unit. Uruguay has nineteen departments (Montevideo (capital) and interior (the other eighteen)).

the interior to Montevideo, with no discrimination by area of origin (rural or urban) is possible. Sex-specific data are given, but age distribution is not available.

The meaning of migration must be defined. The 1963 census registers persons migrating at any time during the 1960–63 period (strictly speaking, this period is of 3.8 years), while the 1975 census registers persons who, five years before, lived in a different place from that of their residence at the time of the census. Thus, neither the return migrants nor, obviously, the deceased during the period are included. As only the total number of migrants is known, if more than one migration occurred throughout the 3.8 or 5 years, it is not registered. Whenever migration is mentioned, reference is made to actual migrants (Niedworok, 1979a). The migratory movements are therefore analysed according to areas and variables mentioned for 1963. Interdepartmental migration towards Montevideo for both 1963 and 1975 is also taken into account, with a view to identifying a trend.

Before studying migration characteristics according to destination, it is useful to have an idea of their volume. The percentage of emigrants in relation to the total original population in 1963 constitutes an approximate measure.

Out of the total population 10 per cent of the women and 7 per cent of the men migrated from the rural area; 2 per cent of the men and 2.6 per cent of the women migrated from the urban area to Montevideo. Therefore towards 1963 both the rural area and the urban area of the interior lost more women than men, as shown in Table 3.

As has been observed in other countries in the area (Elton, 1978), both the rural–urban migrations and the urban–metropolitan migrations are predominantly feminine. Table 4 summarizes the principal characteristics by origin and size of city of destination.

As can be noted, the sex variable does not distinguish the migrants of rural origin by destination. In common with what has been registered for other Latin American countries (Hutchinson, 1963) and taking into

TABLE 3. Distribution of migration by sex according to area of origins and destination (1960–63)

| | Destination | | | | | |
| | Urban interior | | | Montevideo | | |
Origin	Male	Female	Total	Male	Female	Total
Rural	46.5	53.5	100	48.9	51.1	100
Urban interior	49.2	50.8	100	43.6	56.4	100

Source: National Census, 1963 (final data).

25

TABLE 4. Origin and destination of migrants by sex and by area (1960–63)

Origin	Sex	Total	Cities of less than 25,000 inhabitants	Cities of 25,000 inhabitants and more	Montevideo
Rural	Male	100	51	28	21
	Female	100	50	30	20
Urban	Male	100	44	13	41
	Female	100	40	14	46

Source: National Census, 1963 (final data).

account the high level of urbanization of the country (Elizaga, 1970), the percentage of direct migrants to Montevideo (metropolis) from the rural areas is small.

An important volume of migrants flows from the urban interior to Montevideo. When distinguished by the sex this shows that more migrant women than men from the other urban areas choose Montevideo as their destination.

For urban migrants who remain in the interior, practically no variation is registered by sex. Taking this migration as a total, 25 per cent of the men and 26 per cent of the women go to cities with more than 25,000 inhabitants; the rest—75 and 74 per cent respectively—choose smaller cities.

The analysed data shows that 50 per cent of the rural to urban migration is to cities with less than 25,000 inhabitants, while those arriving directly in Montevideo are a minority. At the same time, more than 40 per cent of the urban migration from the interior flows to Montevideo. This may indicate a certain sequence which would point towards a hypothesis of 'migration by stuffing'. In addition, international emigrants leave mostly from Montevideo, as seen in figures of the survey of migration supplemented by the annual mean growth of the population of the capital which, as shown in Table 1(b), is very small.

Emphasis is placed here on 'migration by stuffing', a descriptive term which refers to migration by stages. 'The flow from the land to the large cities and suburbs is not a direct movement but a series of less drastic movements from the land to the village, from the village to the town, from the town to the city and from the city to its suburbs.' (Alberts, 1977, p. 30).

The distribution of migration to Montevideo by sex and age will now be analysed.

26

TABLE 5. Age structure of migrants from the interior to Montevideo by area of origin

| Age-group | Area of origin | | | |
| | Urban | | Rural | |
	Male	Female	Male	Female
0–14	21.1	18.3	15.6	17.2
15–19	15.7	18.8	13.9	17.4
20–24	21.4	20.6	22.9	18.5
25–34	18.8	18.8	21.9	19.1
35–44	9.7	9.2	10.2	10.2
45–54	6.1	6.6	6.7	7.5
55–64	4.1	4.0	4.8	5.4
65 and over	2.9	3.7	4.0	4.7
TOTAL	100.0	100.0	100.0	100.0
30 years and over	30.4	30.9	33.8	35.5

Source: National Census, 1963 (final data).

As shown in Table 5, over 55 per cent of all the subgroups of migrants are between the ages of 15 and 24, the modal age being in the 20–24 range, with the exception of women of rural origin where a more dispersed distribution is found.

The preponderance of the younger ages among the migrants has been verified by numerous studies (Alberts, 1977). This is understandable, as it is the young people who generally have more independence and better chances of obtaining employment. Nevertheless, in relative terms, compared with other Latin American countries, where the modal age is between 15 and 19 years (Alberts, 1977), Uruguayan migrations take place at a later age. To this is added the fact that a high percentage of migrants is 30 years and over (over 30 per cent). As regards differences by sex, there is an over-representation of women in the 15–19 age-group, as can be observed in Table 6.

If the sex ratio of all migrants (separately for urban and rural areas) is taken as an indicator, it can be seen that wherever the ratio is more than unity, males are over-represented (and women are under-represented) in relation to the distribution of the total migration. According to this criterion and leaving aside persons of 0–14 years, who are considered dependent migrants, masculine migration is concentrated in the 20–44 age-group. As regards rural migration, men are the absolute majority for the 20–34 age-group. It therefore seems that migration for labour reasons is more defined for men than for women, as women are concentrated either in the 15–19 age-group or in older age-groups. The concentration of women between 15 and 19 years is very common in the Latin American context and—though on a much smaller scale—is also evident

TABLE 6. Sex ratio of migrants from the interior to Montevideo by age-groups and by area of origin (1960–63)

Age-groups	Origin	
	Urban	Rural
0–14	0.89	0.86
15–19	0.65	0.77
20–24	0.81	1.19
25–34	0.78	1.10
35–44	0.82	0.96
45–54	0.71	0.85
55–64	0.81	0.84
65 and over	0.62	0.82
TOTAL	0.77	0.96

Source: National Census, 1963 (final data).

in Uruguay. The entry of very young women into the labour market as domestic employees is customary. The way in which this takes place is the following: families of rural landowners whose residence—or at least one of their residences—is in Montevideo recruit their domestic staff in the interior, and also often serve at the same time as intermediaries in obtaining domestic employees for purely Montevidean families. A network of recruitment is thus created which favours the migration of young women from the interior.

The evolution of migration between 1963 and 1975 is analysed below. If only interdepartmental migrations are taken into account—without urban–rural breakdown, since the 1975 census does not provide it—it is possible to obtain some type of comparability between the two censuses.

Table 7 shows that in the total interdepartmental migrations, there has been an increase in the choice of Montevideo as the destination. This is independent of the volume of migration to the capital.

TABLE 7. Interdepartmental migration from the rest of country to Montevideo (1960–63 and 1970–75)

Year	Sex	Origin	Destination		
			Total	Rest of country	Montevideo
1963	Male	Interior	100	57	43
	Female	Interior	100	47	53
1975	Male	Interior	100	51	49
	Female	Interior	100	40	60

Source: National Censuses, 1963 (definitive data), 1975 (preliminary sample). (Only three censuses have been undertaken in this century, in 1908, 1963 and 1975.)

The central location of Montevideo as a pole of attraction of interdepartmental migration from the interior is clear. In this respect, the metropolitan orientation of women is maintained.

However, it is important to complete the information with the sex structure of migration to the capital as well as its volume. Between the years 1963 and 1975, a relatively important change in the percentages of men and women arriving in Montevideo took place. At the beginning of the intercensal period 45 per cent were men and 55 per cent women and in 1975 the percentages were 48 and 52 respectively.

An attempt has been made to estimate the changes in the volume of migration towards Montevideo, on the basis of the information available. Assuming that individual displacements are distributed equally over the span of both periods, it is possible to estimate the changes in the volume of migration from the interior to Montevideo, in relation to the total population of the interior.

Migrations to the capital have maintained their volume but their sex composition has changed: there is an increase in the number of men and a decrease in the number of women. In spite of the precariousness of this fact, it is consistent with the information which will be analysed later.

TABLE 8. Proportion of interdepartmental migrations from the rest of the country to Montevideo with regard to the total population of the interior by sex

	Men	Women	Total
1963[1]	3.2	4.2	3.7
1975	3.5	4.1	3.8

1. In order to obtain some comparability of migration volumes, the 1960–63 period figure was estimated according to the following procedure: the original figure was divided by the 1963 census period (3.8 years) and multiplied by the 1975 census period (5 years).

Source: National Censuses, 1963 (definitive data), 1975 (preliminary sample). (Only three censuses have been undertaken in this century, in 1908, 1963 and 1975.)

4 The economically active female population

General trends

The evolution of the economically active female population (EAFP) is interesting in itself. Of equal interest is the way in which it is reflected in changes in the labour-force distribution by sex.

It is possible to observe the growth of the economically active population (EAP) throughout the intercensal period, by sex and by areas.

As can be seen in Table 9, the EAP's growth rate as a whole has been greater than that of the total population and the difference is even more marked with regard to the population between 15 and 64 years (see Table 1(b)).

However, the EAP growth rate differs according to sex: while for men it is less than half that of the total population and more than half that of the 15–64-year-olds, for women the situation is the opposite: the

TABLE 9. Mean annual growth rate (%) of the EAP by sex and by area (1963–75)

	Male	Female	Total
Total	0.22	1.8	0.65
Montevideo	−0.34	1.0	0.10
Interior	0.65	2.9	1.14
Urban[1]	1.47	2.82	1.83
Rural	−0.65	2.83	−0.27

1. The disaggregated data on urban and rural areas for 1963 are from the preliminary sample, since the final data do not show this disaggregation. Comparing them with the totals, the variations between both sources are irrelevant.
Source: National Censuses, 1963 (definitive data and preliminary sample), 1975 (preliminary sample).

EAFP growth rate is more than double that of the total population and that of the 15–64-year-olds.

Considering this growth of the labour force in a context of economic stagnation, it is useful to offer an explanation of the combination of two apparently contradictory situations: (a) international emigration induced by this stagnation, and (b) relative growth of the economically active population.

The concept of 'relative deprivation' helps us understand many of the Uruguayan society's social phenomena.[1] Uruguay's social development was based on a process of economic expansion sustained from the beginning of the century till the mid-1950s. This social development acquires its own dynamics, which continue when the economic factors which made it possible no longer obtain. More important, during the sustained economic prosperity, the population became accustomed to a standard of living and consumption—not only material, but cultural in a wide sense—which cannot be maintained in the new situation of recession. The mechanisms the system generated to meet this demand were diverse. The 'exhaustion of the model' unleashes a massive emigration of particular characteristics. Those who leave the country—statistically speaking—do not do so for motives of strict survival, but rather to maintain certain living standards.

To this one has to add the particular location of the country and, within the country, of Montevideo. The proximity of the Argentine capital—Buenos Aires—a city with which cultural distance is practically non-existent and which has very low unemployment figures—make it very attractive. Moreover, being a far more 'modern' city in the widest sense, it provides for the satisfaction of consumer aspirations which—with the same amount of work—Uruguay does not. 'Relative deprivation' is therefore the main motive force of emigration and the educational levels of emigrants illustrate this point.

It would be convenient to pause briefly here in order to avoid possible contradictions. Emigration has two principal economic reasons. They are the growing deterioration of income and increasing unemployment (the variable which is clearly selective is the level of unemployment: almost 24 per cent of the emigrants as compared with 7 per cent of the

1. Gurr's definition of this concept is: 'The perception on the part of the 'actors' of the discrepancy between the values one expects to receive and those which may be acquired. The expected values (expectations of values) are the means and standard of life one feels entitled to. . . . The axis of the hypothesis resides in the perception of the deprivations: people may be subjectively deprived of the means they expect to receive although to an objective observer they may not appear to be wanting. Similarly, what an observer may consider to be abject poverty or absolute deprivation may not, perforce be unjust and irremediable for him who suffers it. . . . The point of reference of an individual may be his own past condition. . . .'. (Gurr, 1970, p. 25).

national population). Had it not been for the safety-valve of migration, the social consequences of these economic factors would have been catastrophic, mainly because of the generally high level of social development and living standards compared with those of other countries in the region—Argentina excepted. However, these high standards of living provide a fairly wide margin before reaching subsistence level. One must also think in terms of 'social resources'—kinship and friendship—which prevent an abrupt fall to subsistence level.

What has been stated so far attempts to situate Uruguay within the Latin American context, in order to understand the type of emigration occurring, since it is clearly differentiated from the traditional massive migrations in the region. It is at this level that the use of 'relative deprivation' as a concept is considered adequate.

This concept also helps us to understand the increment in the EAP and more particularly the marked growth in the EAFP, principally in the urban areas (95 per cent of the total EAFP towards 1975). Women take up remunerative work to compensate for the increasing deterioration in the family income and to prevent this decreasing income from lowering the standard of living. What is noteworthy is that the increase of female labour—traditionally considered a secondary work-force—occurs in spite of continuing high rates of male unemployment (Prates and Taglioretti, 1980). It is reasonable to suppose that international emigration plays an important role. Given its selectivity as regards sex—chiefly male—and age, young people of active age—emigration signified an important liberation of jobs, which were to be occupied by women.

Furthermore, it is necessary to bear in mind the 'over-tertiarization' of the country and the high levels of education to which women have had access—higher than that of men in the 1975 census. This of course makes them competitive on the labour market. This point will be developed further in the course of the analysis.

Another factor which may have favoured this growth is that when a woman leaves home she partly gives up domestic chores. These, or at least part of them, must be done by someone. Her own departure generates a demand for labour which changes from non-renumerated to remunerated and this substitution acquires particular characteristics.

Yet the general interpretation that has been developed so far (which answers to statistical criteria) does not mean that it is applicable to all women without distinction. The problem of women in the abstract does not exist (De Riz, 1975); rather it is necessary to take into account singularities which cover women from different socio-economic sectors of the population in order to establish more specific hypotheses. In the course of the analysis, therefore, an attempt will be made to point out these different situations.

32

An analysis of the annual mean growth rate of the EAP in relation to certain areas and to that of the potentially active population (Tables 9 and 1 respectively) reveals relative distances between them, which may be considered as indicators of greater—or lesser—occupational possi- bilities: the greater relative distance indicates fewer occupational possibilities. In this way, it can be observed that Montevideo presents the lesser relative distance, both for men and for women. If the rural interior is left aside, since its specific qualities require a more detailed analysis, it is the urban interior which presents the greater relative distances. In the same way, unemployment in the urban interior is somewhat higher for men than for women: 9 and 7 per cent respectively. Interdepartmental migration towards Montevideo may be considered basically urban (because of the weight of the urban population in the total of the interior and the low percentages of rural migration to

TABLE 10. EAP structure by sex and by area (%)

| | 1963 | | | 1975 | | |
	Male	Female	Total	Male	Female	Total
Total	75.1	24.9	100	71.5	28.5	100
Montevideo	69.0	31.0	100	65.6	34.5	100
Interior total	80.8	19.2	100	76.3	23.7	100
Urban	74.8	25.2	100	71.7	28.3	100
Rural	91.0	9.0	100	87.0	13.0	100

Source: National Censuses, 1963 and 1975 (preliminary samples).

Montevideo.) Moreover the relative male increase is consistent in changes in the sex structure of this migration. Furthermore, unemploy- ment in Montevideo is lower for men: 6.4 per cent for men and 7 per cent for women.

The way in which the differential increments of activity reflect on the EAP sex structure can be observed in Table 10.

As expected, the weight for women in the EAP increases considerably: 3.6 per cent. This means that in Montevideo the EAFP is more than a third of the EAP (Figure 2). Bearing in mind the urban and rural distribution and comparing the information with that of Argentina, which has equally high female activity rates and which is similar to Uruguay in its social factors, it may be observed that towards 1960 female participation in the Uruguayan EAP is somewhat higher, but that towards 1970 this participation shifts away from the pattern in Argentina. However, the increase in the relative weight of EAFP in EAP common to both countries must be emphasized. (Table 11).

33

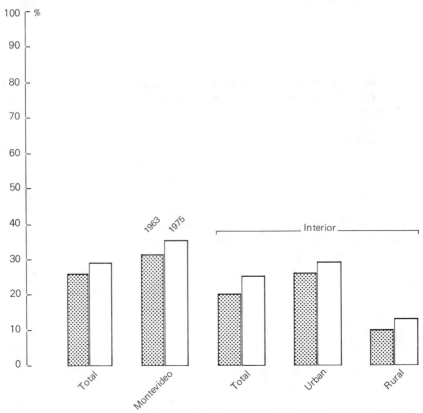

FIG. 2. Proportion of EAFP in the EAP by area, 1963 and 1975 (after National Censuses, 1963 and 1975 (preliminary samples)).

TABLE 11. Argentina and Uruguay: EAFP percentages over EAP by area[1]

	Towards 1960			Towards 1970		
	Urban	Rural	Total	Urban	Rural	Total
Argentina	23.9	12.2	24.0	27.5	14.1	24.8
Uruguay	28.6	9.0	24.9	31.6	13.0	28.5

1. The Argentine data are taken from the 1960 and 1970 censuses and the Uruguayan from 1963 and 1975.

Source: Argentina: Recchini de Lattes (1980); Uruguay: National Censuses, 1963 (definitive data), 1975 (preliminary sample). (Only three censuses have been undertaken this century, in 1908, 1963 and 1975.)

Female participation in economic activity by age

The general tendency of female activities and the way they are reflected in a differential distribution of the labour force by sex has been studied. We shall now analyse the evolution of the levels of activity by age.

34

In order to distinguish Montevideo from the urban interior which has what may be called two 'particular' labour markets, it was found necessary to use data from the 1975 census. This does not include the category 'seeking work for the first time'. For reasons of comparability, these were also eliminated from the 1963 census figures and this affects particularly the specific rates for the younger age-groups.

An emigration consisting principally of young men liberates occupational positions and leads to a greater incorporation of women into the labour market. The rate of activity for both sexes is shown in Figure 3. Late incorporation into the labour market and the continuation of activities until more advanced ages are features common to both sexes which should be emphasized. The first is related to the prolongation of schooling, while the second is a consequence of the economic situation of which one important effect is the drop in the purchasing power of pensions. The two phenomena may be interrelated: the longer activity results in the non-liberation of occupational positions and a decrease in possibilities for younger persons to enter the labour market.

Some differences between areas should be emphasized. As Montevideo has lower initial rates, the prolongation of activity is more clearly evident: the rates for the capital for age 45 (in 1975) are quite similar to those for the urban interior.

The most outstanding feature in the rates of female activity is the

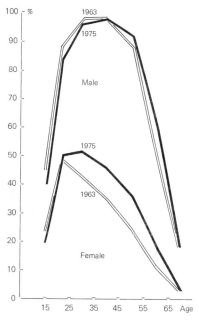

FIG. 3(a). Montevideo: rates of activity by age and sex, 1963 and 1975 (after National Censuses, 1963 (definitive data), 1975 (preliminary sample), as in Appendix Table 1).

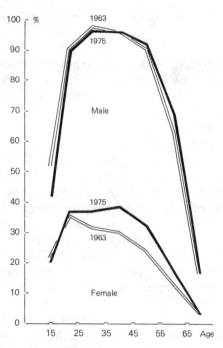

FIG. 3(b). Urban interior: rates of activity by age and sex, 1963 and 1975 (after National Censuses, 1963 (definitive data), 1975 (preliminary sample), as in Appendix Table 1).

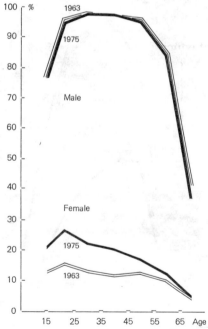

FIG. 3(c). Rural interior: rates of activity by age and sex, 1963 and 1975 (after National Censuses, 1963 (definitive data), 1975 (preliminary sample), as in Appendix Table 1).

36

permanence of women in the labour market even during child-bearing ages when marked decreases are normally registered. In this respect, the difference between Montevideo and the urban interior is striking. While the former shows higher levels but a greater drop starting at the age of 25, the latter shows lower levels but greater permanence. This may be related to the more modern characteristics of Montevideo, where activities which are preponderantly outside the home, make work and the bringing up of children incompatible (Pantelides, 1976). In the cities of the interior which are smaller there are, among other things, closer relationships between the inhabitants and women count on greater support to work away from home.

The evolution of the rates of activity shown in Figure 3a confirm the relation established between the departure of men from the labour market and their substitution by women. In fact, Montevideo shows a reduction in the rates of male activity for the 20–34 age-group, especially in the 20–24 age-group.

However, some explanation must be given about what appears to be a replacement of men by women in the labour market. As will be seen later, the particular configuration of the Uruguayan labour market favours the integration of women. This labour market, with a large tertiary sector, is characterized in Montevideo by a relative increase of middle-level, traditionally female, occupations for which formal schooling in humanities is an important channel of access. To this is added the fact that the high supply of work for this type of demand— given the increase of education and the increase in its levels—influences the level of remunerations which makes women's competivity relative. This is particularly relevant for the younger ages but also applies to all active women. It would seem that the marked increase in female economic participation is the result of the confluence of favourable supply factors and special conditions of demand.

The relative increases in the rates of activity in the rural interior, especially for the younger ages, are shown in Figure 3c. While the levels of activity were relatively steady for all ages towards 1963, the younger ages show a greater increase in 1975. This is accompanied by a decreasing tendency in masculine activity in the same age-groups. As a result of the economic crisis faced by the small rural farms, where the majority of the rural population are to be found, paid workers have frequently been dispensed with and women are now carrying out their work; EAFP shows a considerable increase in the category of 'non-renumerated family worker'. The hypothesis could be advanced that should these differential tendencies in the incorporation into the labour market continue, the migratory patterns by sex will be affected. Unfortunately, data allowing for the observation of the characteristics of rural migration around 1975 are not available.

Female participation in economic activity by age and by marital status

Marital status is one of the factors with considerable influence on the economic participation of women. Although Uruguay follows this pattern and the rates of participation show important differences according to this variable, these are smaller in relation to the Latin American context, where differences in participation among single women are several times greater than those for married women and can reach the ratio of 5:1 in the 20–24 age-group (Kirsch, 1975).

Figure 4 shows how the curves of participation are affected by age and marital status. There has been a relatively even increase in each different status, albeit with differential characteristics. While single women, widows, separated and divorced women show lower rates towards 1975 in the younger ages, married women increase their participation at these ages. It is here, in fact, that greater increases are manifest and this can be partially accounted for by the fact that their initial rates are low, and they have greater possibilities of increasing them. It is, however, also a consequence of the necessity of the family group to increase its income to compensate for the loss of purchasing power. It should be pointed out that the highest levels appear in the child-bearing ages (25–44 years). It is also worth noting that although the rates of single women and particularly of widows, divorced and separated women in the regions start at high levels of activity, they still increase.

The fact that the rates of activity of the three groups are so high within the Latin American context, while at the same time increasing in a relatively homogeneous pattern during the intercensal period, with married women showing the higher relative increase, indicates the independence of women and a favourable social attitude towards their participation in the labour market. In this sense, the cultural factors, taken in the widest sense, are central and more especially the social and civil legislation which dates from the first decades of this century. In addition, women have been integrated to a large extent into the urban labour market, since the beginning of the century. This implies integration in a heterogeneous market that could be called 'cosmopolitan' which makes the positive attitude towards the integration of women into the labour market a routine affair at the social level.

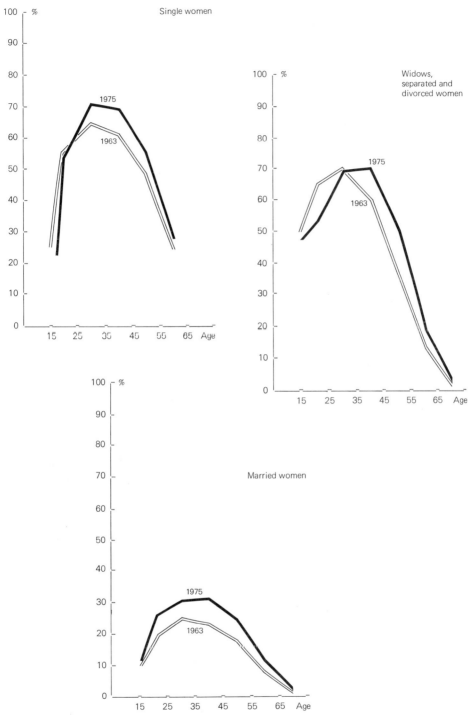

FIG. 4. Uruguay: female rates of activity by age and by marital status, 1963 and 1975 (after National Censuses, 1963 (definitive data), 1975 (preliminary sample), as in Appendix Table 2).

Female participation in economic activity by educational levels

Formal education has proved to be an important intervening variable in the participation of women in the labour market.

In this respect, it has been observed that in many Latin American countries, the educational levels of the EAFP are higher than those of the economically active male population (EAMP) (Kirsch, 1975). This may indicate two different phenomena: on the one hand, that women with higher educational levels are more predisposed to enter the labour market and, on the other, that there are higher requirements for women than for men, in other words, that there is a clear discrimination against women.

As shown in Table 12, Uruguay follows the regional pattern: women have higher educational levels than men. It should be pointed out that—considering the extension of education in this country—the educational levels of the Uruguayan EAP surpass those of the majority of the countries of the region and are accompanied by the fact that the levels of female activity in Uruguay are higher than the regional ones (only Chile for both sexes and Panama as regards women, show higher percentages of over seven years of schooling).

This quite particular characteristic must be analysed bearing in mind the marked 'over-tertiarization' of the Uruguayan labour market. It is not possible to ignore the combined influence of the expansion of formal education and the hypertrophy of the tertiary sector. As has been pointed out, education begins to expand in reply to a constantly growing

TABLE 12. EAMP and EAFP structure by educational level. Total of the country, 1963 and 1975 (%)

	EAMP		EAFP	
	1963	1975	1963	1975
Illiterates	9.3	5.2	7.3	4.0
Some primary	46.8	35.1	37.2	24.8
Completed primary	23.8	29.0	27.1	27.9
Secondary	10.9	13.0	14.2	16.8
Pre-university and university	4.8	8.2	5.3	12.5
Teaching and others	0.7	1.6	6.1	7.9
Middle-level technical	3.6	7.9	2.7	6.0
TOTAL	100.0	100.0	100.0	100.0

Source: National Census, 1963 (final data).

40

occupational market, but continues to expand further on its own impetus. In this new situation, the pressure of the educated sectors to attain their aspirations, produce an inverse ratio: the growth of the tertiary sector in order to satisfy the demand of educated sectors of the population.

In this context, women benefit, as they have at their disposal occupational positions traditionally considered as female. In a certain sense, given a situation of economic crisis, women go out to work because they are educated and because a market exists for their type of work.

Unfortunately, sources of information do not allow for a detailed analysis of the differentials of education by sex in EAP but are available

TABLE 13. EAP by sex and by educational level. Total of the country, 1963 and 1975 (%)

	EAP					
	1963			1975		
	Male	Female	Total	Male	Female	Total
Illiterates	79.5	20.5	100.0	76.9	23.1	100.0
Some primary	79.3	20.7	100.0	78.2	21.8	100.0
Primary completed	72.8	27.2	100.0	72.5	27.5	100.0
Secondary	70.0	30.0	100.0	66.3	33.7	100.0
Pre-university and university	73.2	26.8	100.0	62.4	37.6	100.0
Teaching and others	26.4	73.6	100.0	34.0	66.0	100.0
Middle-level technical	80.1	19.9	100.0	76.9	23.1	100.0
TOTAL	75.2	24.8	100.0	71.8	28.2	100.0

Source: National Census, 1963 (final data).

for the distribution by sex and by level (Appendix Table 6). In fact, if the total distribution by sex is taken as a limit, it is possible to observe those levels which—by exceeding the total percentage—indicate a feminine over-representation.

In the first place, it should be said that technical levels are apparently 'masculine' and teaching levels 'feminine'. As regards the other levels, it should be pointed out that while in 1963 women are over-represented at the level of completed primary schooling, in 1975 they are so at the secondary level (Table 13). The remarkable feature is, undoubtedly, the marked relative increase evident at the pre-university and university level: while it exceeded the total percentage by 8 per cent in 1963, in 1975 it surpasses it by 33 per cent. This fact is consistent with the modality adopted for the insertion of women into a labour market of particular characteristics, which will be analysed.

41

Economically active female population in the different branches of activity

Given that women's participation in the labour market depends on the evolution of economic activity as a whole, data are given on the evolution and structure of the total economically active population (EAP) (Figures 5 and 6). It must be noted that in order to compare the categories in both censuses, it was necessary to apply the disaggregation to the three digits method which does not take in the urban–rural distinction. Therefore, information for Montevideo and the interior of the country is given as a total. Given the importance of the rural area from the point of view of migration, some comparable information will be retrieved later for this area.

The outstanding feature of the data in Table 14 is a loss in the relative importance of the primary sector of EAP in the interior, particularly low in national terms (19.4 and 16.6 per cent in 1963 and 1975 respectively) within the context of Latin America. At the national level there is a relative improvement in the tertiary sector (50.8 per cent in 1963 and

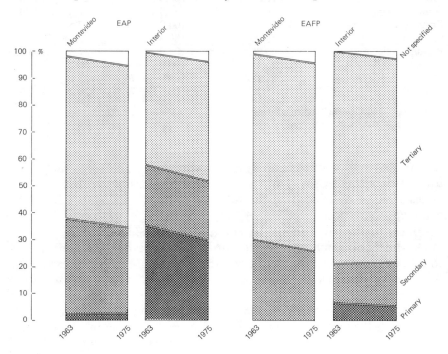

FIG. 5. Distribution of the EAP and EAFP by sectors of the economy 1963 and 1975 (after National Census, 1963 (definitive data), 1975 (census sample)).

42

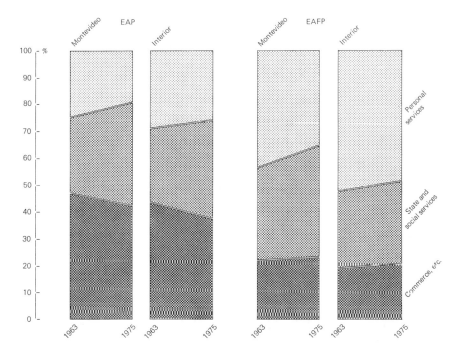

Fig. 6. Distribution of EAP and EAFP in the tertiary sector by aggregated branches of activity 1963 and 1975 (after National Census, 1963 (definitive data), 1975 (census sample)).

51.7 per cent in 1975). This tendency is shared with several countries of the area and results from the relative growth in the interior, for it remains unchanged in Montevideo. The secondary sector loses relative weight on the national level (28.6 per cent in 1963 and 27.4 per cent in 1975) and this is a reflection of two opposite tendencies: a decrease in Montevideo and a small increase in the interior. It does not, however, seem wise to draw conclusions given the relative increase in the category of 'activities not well specified'.

The women's work-force in Uruguay shows a pronounced 'tertiarization'. In spite of this, although the tertiary sector for EAFP is greater than for EAP, the figures for EAFP, unlike those for EAP, show no increase during the intercensal period.

Although the EAFP retains the same relative weight, its internal structure has undergone important changes. Interesting variations are observed when taking into consideration: (a) those branches more closely related to the diversification of the economy, (b) services of collective consumption which are related to the standard of living of the population, and (c) those of individual consumption (Recchini de Lattes, 1980). A relative drop in personal services is evident for both Montevideo and the interior and this is also present at the EAP level. The item 'state and social services' shows the greatest increase, with

43

TABLE 14. Structure of EAP and EAFP, by area and sector of the economy: 1963 and 1975 (%)[1]

	EAP				EAFP			
	Montevideo		Interior		Montevideo		Interior	
	1963	1975	1963	1975	1963	1975	1963	1975
Primary sector	2.1	2.1	35.6	29.0	0.3	0.4	6.7	5.4
Secondary sector	35.3	32.3	22.2	23.2	28.7	26.1	20.8	19.4
Tertiary sector	60.9	60.8	41.6	44.0	69.6	69.6	72.2	72.9
(a)[2]	(28.7)	(25.9)	(18.6)	(17.0)	(16.4)	(16.8)	(14.7)	(16.2)
(b)	(17.5)	(23.7)	(11.4)	(16.1)	(23.3)	(29.2)	(19.9)	(22.9)
(c)	(14.7)	(11.2)	(11.6)	(10.9)	(29.9)	(23.6)	(37.6)	(33.8)
Activities not specified	1.7	4.8	0.7	3.8	1.4	3.9	0.3	2.3
TOTAL	100.0	100.0	100.0	100.0	100.0	100.0	100.0	100.0

1. 1963: Population age 10 years and more; 1975: population age 12 years and more.
2. (a) Commerce, restaurants and hotels; transport, storage and communication; financial services, insurances, services to enterprises.
   (b) State and social services.
   (c) Personal services.

Source: National Censuses, 1963 (definitive data), 1975 (census sample).

stronger emphasis in Montevideo than in the interior; at the same time, the aggregate of the rest of the branches shows a more pronounced increase in the interior than in Montevideo, in contrast with the drop for EAP in both areas.

Data are given in Table 15 for the total branches of activity, taking into consideration the annual mean growth rates (per cent) together with distribution of the increases by different branches, both for EAFP and for EAP. The distribution of the increases reveals the areas in which women are most frequently incorporated.

It can be observed that 'state and social services' is the branch which absorbs the highest increase both for EAP and EAFP in Montevideo and in the interior of the country, but with important differences in the percentages of absorption.

In Montevideo the percentage of integration for this category amounts to 196.1 per cent of EAP, with its counterpart in an absolute decrease in most of the remaining branches—except in the primary sector which for Montevideo is irrelevant— and 'activities not specified'. This distribution evidently results from a decrease in male activity. Male participation has less weight in all branches including 'state and social services', as shown by the annual mean growth rate where EAFP is higher than EAP.

The increase of EAFP in this branch should be related to the information as a whole. Since no decreases are registered for the different categories—except in 'personal services'—a percentage of 70.2 in the increase in 'state and social services' corroborates the previous statement. In statistical terms, the massive incorporation of women—particularly in Montevideo—is evident in occupations in the middle sectors. The next highest percentage corresponds to 'financial services, etc.'. The aggregate of the tertiary sector—eliminating 'personal services'—shows that approximately 90 per cent of the increase in feminine activities in Montevideo is to be found in this sector.

In the secondary sector, manufacturing industry—traditionally a more 'feminine' industry than the others—is the only branch which absorbs a noteworthy percentage of the increase and this results in an increase of the female labour force in this branch over the male labour force. It is convenient to interpret the evolution of 'personal services' together with developments in the interior, as it constitutes a good indicator of important differences between the two 'particular' markets.

The evolution of the primary sector is studied through an analysis of the rural area. In the interior, the growth of 'state and social services' is relatively greater than in 1963—when compared with that for Montevideo; however, for both EAP and EAFP it absorbs a smaller percentage of the total increase.

Taking into account the annual mean growth rate in this area, the

TABLE 15. Annual mean growth rates (%) of EAP and EAFP and distribution of growth of EAP and EAFP by area and by branches of activity[1] (1963–75) (%)

Branches of activity	Annual mean growth rates				Distribution of growth			
	Montevideo		Interior		Montevideo		Interior	
	EAP	EAFP	EAP	EAFP	EAP	EAFP	EAP	EAFP
Agriculture, forestry, hunting and fishing	0.38	3.59	−0.70	0.74	2.6	1.2	−20.9	1.8
Mining and quarrying	−1.39	−17.24	−0.64	−17.24	−0.2	0.0	−0.2	0.0
Manufacturing	−0.36	0.29	1.74	2.00	−32.2	6.5	23.3	15.7
Electricity, gas, water	−2.16	0.95	1.44	−2.87	−13.7	0.6	1.8	−0.4
Construction	−0.40	4.75	0.83	−3.39	−6.1	1.1	5.2	−0.2
Commerce, restaurants and hotels	−0.69	0.55	0.92	3.35	−34.9	5.6	10.0	17.5
Transport, storage and communication	−0.54	3.58	−0.71	3.69	−12.6	5.4	−3.0	2.3
Financial establishments, insurance, services to enterprises	−0.44	3.11	−0.67	1.75	−7.0	8.5	−1.0	0.7
State and social services	2.89	3.09	3.99	3.67	196.1	70.2	51.7	31.9
Personal services	−1.99	−0.87	0.51	1.57	−84.5	−19.8	5.4	22.3
Activities not specified	8.54	8.36	12.47	14.61	92.5	20.8	27.6	8.3
TOTAL					100.0	100.0	100.0	100.0

1. Increases in each branch of activity related to total is obtained with the following formula:

$$I_r = \frac{P_{r75} - P_{r63}}{P_{t75} - P_{t63}}$$

where P_r is the population in the respective branch and P_t is the total or feminine economically active population depending on EAP or EAFP.
Source: National Censuses, 1963 (definitive data), 1975 (census sample).

male labour force gains over the female one. This differential tendency corroborates one of the hypotheses presented: the highest replacement mobility is to be found in Montevideo, where most of the emigration originates and this is the reason for the increase of female activity in this branch compared with male activity. In the remaining branches of the tertiary sector, female labour registers an advance over the male work-force.

Manufacturing industry presents a similar picture and it also absorbs an important percentage of the intercensal growth for both EAP and EAFP. This is a different situation from that in Montevideo since industry is growing in the interior at least from the point of view of the work-force. This results from the increase in the processing of products of the primary sector—basically fish, hides and textiles—which generated employment for both women—artisanal spinning of wool and processing and packaging of fish—and men. At the same time, the building of hydroelectric dams and the growth in the construction industry for the building of seaside resort dwellings, has generated a demand for a male work-force.

The evolution of 'personal services' during the intercensal period will be analysed. Multiple factors merit a particular and comparative treatment of this branch of activity as between Montevideo and the interior. Distinctly different trends are observed in the two areas. In Montevideo the absolute figures decrease and in the interior they increase for both EAP and EAFP. Secondly, within the EAFP, besides its loss in relative importance, this category represents almost a quarter of Montevideo's total and a third of the interior's total female population of working age. Thirdly, due to their socio-economic origin and the dispersion of the services, the workers have fewer means to defend their general working conditions. This situation is clearly different from the case of manufacturing industries, where the workers have the same socio-economic origin, but where they are more concentrated at the workplace.

Table 16 shows the development of 'domestic service' and its relative

TABLE 16. Annual mean growth rate (%) of domestic service and proportion of it within 'personal services' by area, 1963 and 1975

	Montevideo		Interior	
	1963	1975	1963	1975
Annual mean growth rate (%)	−0.22		3.01	
Proportion of 'domestic service' within 'personal services' (%)	76.8	82.2	69.6	92.0

Source: National Census, 1963 (definitive data), 1975 (census sample).

importance within the category. This justifies centring the analysis on it in order to formulate hypotheses which reveal the important differences between Montevideo and the interior.

The interpretation centres on the different costs of these services in Montevideo and the interior. Various factors contribute to the establishment of the hypothesis of cost differentials. Generally, it may be maintained that the metropolitan society is more modern than that of the interior, the difference in population density being one of the reasons. Montevideo has 45 per cent of the total population of the country in a territory which represents 0.3 per cent of the total territory of Uruguay. The majority of the population in the interior is urban, but its urban centres are small. Therefore, the type of relations established in both areas differ greatly: in Montevideo arrangements tend to be contractual, whereas in the interior they tend to be informal. These differences lead to a possibility of much lower pay in the interior than in Montevideo. To the above factors must also be added others of a different nature. The size of the cities in the interior means that the cost of transportation to the place of work is nil. In Montevideo, popular neighbourhoods are some distance from the places where domestic employees work and public transport is very expensive. To this must be added the cost for transport which is borne by the employer. The possibility that the employee lives under the same roof as her employers is greater in the interior than in Montevideo since houses in Montevideo are on the average smaller than those in the interior. Because it is a more modern society, a greater value is placed on independence and it is not only the demand for a living-in domestic service that has decreased, but also the supply. All these factors must in turn be related to the drop in family incomes, which is reflected in a reduction of an expensive and dispensable service—a few days a week for the heavier tasks—if not in its total elimination. This allows us to assume that the total number of contracted hours of paid domestic work diminished considerably between 1963 and 1975.

However, household work is not only the cleaning and cooking which may be done by domestic help. It also includes other almost exclusively feminine tasks such as making and mending clothes, knitting, etc. Although men may help in other daily tasks they do not frequently do so in these. On the basis of the household surveys carried out in Montevideo in 1975, it appears that 80 per cent of the women who were working worked 30 hours or more a week (59 per cent worked more than 40 hours per week). It therefore seems reasonable to suppose that a demand for work which it is difficult to perform at home has been generated. It is important to note that these are less continuous tasks than the daily domestic chores and, therefore, less remunerative in terms of the monthly income. In the same way, women belonging to the popular sectors who do unqualified work receive low remuneration. When away from their homes, they have additional expenses—especially for payment of childcare centres, as such generalized services are not free. It is therefore more convenient for women to do paid work in their homes, i.e. knitting or sewing.

Finally, there has apparently been a change in demand which has provoked a complementary change in supply; thus, domestic service decreases in spite of the large number of women in paid work and, at the same time, a growth of 'activities not specified'. This seems to indicate a fairly large number of women who do paid work in their own homes and who—for legal reasons—do not clearly specify the type of work they do.

Women from the middle sectors who go out to paid work not only generate a demand for unqualified or semi-qualified work but for qualified work as well. A good example is the private child-care centres, generally staffed with specialized personnel or, at least, with persons having higher formal education. This is a service which has grown considerably during the intercensal period, and which clearly falls within the 'state and social services' category.

The weight of the services sector in the EAFP is the reason for the particular attention paid here to its evolution. At the same time, the attempt to present interpretative hypotheses for the evolution of the 'state and social services' together with those for 'personal services' is a response to the central position they occupy in the reorganization of the sector. The former absorbs the largest percentage of the increase in female economic participation in both Montevideo and (to a lesser extent) in the interior. In this sense, the different tendency which both branches show in Montevideo and in the interior should be noted: in Montevideo 'personal services' decrease their relative weight, in comparison with the beginning of the period, by 21 per cent, while the interior does so by only 10 per cent; at the same time 'state and social services' increase their relative weight by 25 and 15 per cent respectively. Should these tendencies continue, differences between Montevideo and the interior will be more accentuated with all that this implies from the point of view of the migratory process, particularly concerning selectivity.

Comparable information on the *rural* areas will now be analysed. Although the merging of the different branches of activity was necessary in some cases—as can be seen in Table 17—some interesting hypotheses may be put forward.

The pronounced decrease in activities in the primary sector is worth noting. Since female participation in absolute figures remains unchanged, it is male participation which shows a notable decrease, as shown in Table 9.

Land is exploited in the rural area in two ways: the first is extensive

TABLE 17. Structure, annual mean growth rate (%) and distribution of growth (%) of rural EAP and EAFP by branch of activity (1963–75)

| | Structure | | | | Annual mean growth rate (%) | | Distribution of growth (%) | |
| | EAP | | EAFP | | | | | |
	1963	1975	1963	1975	EAP	EAFP	EAP[1]	EAFP
Agriculture, forestry, hunting, and fishing	80.0	73.0	38.2	27.9	−1.0	0.0	358.1	0.0
Rest of the branches[2]	12.0	13.9	16.4	22.6	1.07	5.27	−65.1	39.3
State and social services	4.9	5.8	16.4	14.4	1.30	1.57	−32.6	8.9
Personal services	3.1	4.8	28.9	32.2	3.55	3.57	−65.1	41.1
Activities not specified	0.0	2.4	0.0	2.9	15.71	8.62	−95.3	10.7
TOTAL	100.0	100.0	100.0	100.0			−100.0	100.0

1. As rural EAP decreases, the minus signs mean a decrease.
2. See Table 15.
Source: National Censuses, 1963 and 1975 (preliminary samples).

and predominates in spatial terms; the second is intensive and represents a minority. The first is characterized by a high level of expulsion in general and for females in particular—when a woman leaves, so does the family. The second is less expulsory with a population more evenly balanced by sex (the sex ratio of population by size of the rural exploitations in 1970 showed that farms with over 5,000 ha had an index of 232.5 while for those with 1–9 ha of land the index was 110.3 (Niedworok and Prates, 1979)). It is at the level of this group of rural population—the small rural landowners or tenants—that the evolution of rural EAFP should be interpreted.

The landowners—or tenants—of small rural farms which to some extent make up the middle rural sectors have great difficulty in absorbing the impact of an economic crisis. Generally, these farms are close to cities or urban centres.[1] Confronted with a reduction in income, the women try to find some kind of remunerated activity and the cities or urban centres provide this possibility. It is in the category of 'personal services' that the higher percentage of distribution of the increase occurs. At the same time, although the data cannot be accepted as definitive, because of difficulties as regards their comparability, this nevertheless can be taken as a tendency. The 'manufacturing industry' (29 per cent) is the next most important branch in the distribution of increase. This may be seen from two points of view: the growth of artisanal production—basically spinning and knitting of woollen garments—generates a demand for a female work-force; and secondly, the entry into the urban labour market of women who do paid work at home. In this respect, it has been observed that in Canelones—a department which adjoins Montevideo and has a high proportion of rural population—a large number of women from small rural farms enter urban work.[2] Work is often given to them through a distributor in the zone. They assemble or knit garments by machine or by hand and are as it were self-employed (the increment of this category will be seen later). Given that this system is considered very expensive and that there is plenty of female labour available in the urban area, one can get an idea of the very low rates at which these women are paid.

Women take on this work because they need to supplement their income. They cannot, however, leave the farm, for this would mean neglecting the tasks traditionally carried out by them in a small rural exploitation. These tasks, though not remunerated, have a direct economic bearing on farming yields.

1. Montevideo has a neighbouring department—Canelones—which is an intensive exploitation area, and which provides food for Montevideo.
2. The author is now doing research on the characteristics of the integration into the labour market of women who live on small farms.

Finding themselves confronted with the need to increase their income, women are obliged to work for pay and the place they have found—or made for themselves—is mainly at the urban labour market level.

The economically active female population in the different categories of occupation

As can be seen in Table 18, in all areas and for both EAP and EAFP, the 'employer' category shows a decrease in relative weight. On the other hand, the 'self-employed' category shows an important increase, except for EAFP in the urban interior. At the same time, the relative weight of the category 'salaried employees and wage earners' has dropped for EAP. The category EAFP increases in weight in the urban interior, while dropping in Montevideo and in a pronounced manner in the rural interior. In the same way the rural interior shows a pronounced growth in the relative weight of the category 'unpaid family workers' for EAFP.

An analysis of the rural interior and a study of all the data on EAFP as well as that for EAP allows for several interpretative hypotheses. The higher relative weight of the 'unpaid family worker' within the internal structure of EAFP is accompanied by a high annual mean growth rate which absorbs 42 per cent of the total growth of EAFP. The absolute decrease in the categories of 'employer' and 'salaried employees and wage-earners' for EAP is considered together with the absolute growth in the category of 'self-employed workers'. The differences between these figures and those for EAFP, reveals the trend in EAMP.

On the basis of this it is possible to conclude that the situation of economic stagnation has forced a group of small rural producers to dispense with salaried workers. This accounts for the decrease in 'employers' and 'salaried employees and wage-earners' and the growth in 'self-employed workers'. However, the amount of work needed for the exploitation of the farm remains unchanged. It is therefore women who contribute and this is the cause for the increase in EAFP for the category of 'unpaid family workers'. In reality, women would simply be adding other work to the traditional work they perform on the farm but, in the new situation, they are seen as 'workers', since they, in fact, replace salaried workers. This may have future implications for the re-evaluation of the economic importance of women on rural farms, which might lead to them being considered as workers by reason of their traditional or 'natural' tasks on the farm.

This new approach to the economic activity of women in the rural

TABLE 18(a). EAP and EAFP by area and category of occupation, 1963 and 1975: structure (%)

Category of occupation	Montevideo				Urban interior				Rural interior			
	EAP		EAFP		EAP		EAFP		EAP		EAFP	
	1963	1975	1963	1975	1963	1975	1963	1975	1963	1975	1963	1975
Employers	7.6	5.4	3.4	2.5	8.1	4.8	3.3	2.2	12.4	6.0	4.5	0.9
Self-employed workers	11.6	14.9	14.1	15.5	16.7	20.8	25.5	24.0	25.2	31.5	25.0	27.9
Salaried employees and wage-earners	80.5	79.1	82.1	81.0	74.5	73.2	70.2	71.8	54.7	53.7	64.1	54.9
Unpaid family workers	0.3	0.6	0.4	1.0	0.7	1.2	1.0	2.0	7.7	8.8	6.4	16.3
TOTAL	100.0	100.0	100.0	100.0	100.0	100.0	100.0	100.0	100.0	100.0	100.0	100.0

Source: Niedworok (1979), National Censuses 1963 and 1975 (preliminary samples).

TABLE 18(b). EAP and EAFP by area and category of occupation, 1963 and 1975: annual mean growth rates (%)

Category of occupation	Montevideo		Urban interior		Rural interior	
	EAP	EAFP	EAP	EAFP	EAP	EAFP
	1963 1975	1963 1975	1963 1975	1963 1975	1963 1975	1963 1975
Employers	-2.83	-1.57	-2.64	-0.69	-6.13	-9.58
Self-employed workers	2.28	1.96	3.66	2.17	1.74	3.66
Salaried employees and wage-earners	0.01	1.01	1.64	2.88	-0.35	1.42
Unpaid family workers	6.31	7.84	5.58	7.73	0.95	9.58

Source: National Censuses, 1963 and 1975 (preliminary samples).

TABLE 18(c). EAP and EAFP by area and category of occupation 1963 and 1975: distribution of growth (%)

Category of occupation	Montevideo		Urban interior		Rural interior	
	EAP	EAFP	EAP	EAFP	EAP	EAFP
	1963 1975	1963 1975	1963 1975	1963 1975	1963 1975	1963 1975
Employers	−122.0	−4.1	−9.3	−0.7	305.2	−8.5
Self-employed workers	200.0	25.9	38.7	19.9	−265.8	35.6
Salaried employees and wage-earners	3.7	73.1	67.6	76.3	−102.6	30.5
Unpaid family workers	18.3	5.1	3.0	4.5	−42.1	42.4
TOTAL	100.0	100.0	100.0	100.0	−100.0[1]	100.0[1]

1. As EAP decreases, minus signs mean decrease.
Source: National Censuses, 1963 and 1975 (preliminary samples).

area requires the general hypothesis to be specified: women have gained a work space in the rural labour market, but although this work indirectly avoids a reduction in the family income, it is not directly remunerated. As regards their incorporation into the urban labour market, data would corroborate the following hypothesis: although it does not necessarily have to be urban, there is consistency in the fact that 66 per cent of the increase in EAFP is absorbed by the categories 'self-employed workers' and 'salaried employees and wage-earners'.

In the urban interior—from which the category of 'unpaid family worker' was eliminated because of its low relative weight—the mean annual growth rates show a decrease in the category 'employer', accompanied by an increase in 'self-employed workers'.

Because of the differences between EAP and EAFP, the incorporation of men into this occupational category is considerable and the way in which its relative weight increases in EAP has already been seen. Given the heterogeneity of situations which this category covers, detailed hypotheses cannot be put forward. Nevertheless, and bearing in mind the distribution of the growth by branches of activity, it seems reasonable to maintain that this increase reflects the restricted occupational possibilities which would induce men in particular to find a place for themselves in the labour market. This comes close to being 'masked unemployment'.

As regards women, 'salaried employees and wage-earners' shows the greatest absolute growth and this category also absorbs 76 per cent of the intercensal increase, indicating a tendency towards the 'salarization' of EAFP.

As for Montevideo—once the category of 'unpaid family worker' was eliminated because of its low relative weight—the evolution of EAP and EAFP from the point of view of the annual mean growth rate is similar to that of the urban interior. One feature of the 'salaried employees and wage-earning' group is the annual mean growth rate for EAP which is almost nil (for women it is 1.01 per cent). This is accompanied by a growth in the number of 'self-employed workers'. This category absorbs not only almost all the intercensal growth but also the decrease in the category 'employer'. When considering the distribution of growth by branches of activity, with a high percentage in 'state and social services' a difference may be established between the levels for urban interior and Montevideo. In Montevideo, there may be a tendency towards independent work for men, as a result of the deterioration of salaries which does not necessarily reflect an economic decline in statistical terms (the existence of 'self-employed workers' with a low income is not denied).

As a counterpart, the growth of the number of women in the category of 'salaried employees and wage-earners', which absorbs 73 per cent of the intercensal growth of EAFP, may be related to an implicit form of salary discrimination in the sense that women move to lower-paid jobs. Bearing in mind the process of the devaluation of education already described, women would be competing in a market where salaries are low, which is important as an intervening factor setting the limits of competitive conditions.

The economically active female population in different occupations

Before analysing the evolution of EAP and EAFP by occupation, one should note the difficulties with the data. The high percentage in the category of 'workers not classifiable by occupations' calls for care in reading the results of the preliminary sample of the 1975 census. In this respect, it seems reasonable to suppose that the redistribution of this item would fundamentally affect the lower categories and create greater difficulties for their coding.

None the less, these data are still useful, since if the recent assumptions are correct, the evolution of the occupations related to average socio-economic levels, which play a central role in the general context of this work, may be observed.

When adding together the first three categories (see Table 19 and also Figures 7, 8(a) and 8(b)), it can be seen that Montevideo presents opposing tendencies: while its relative weight for EAP drops from 29.5 to 27.9 per cent of the total, for EAFP it increases considerably from 32.8 per cent in 1963 to 35.4 per cent in 1975. These figures indicate that: women have become mobile through replacement, particularly in those occupations corresponding to the middle sectors, where education constitutes an important channel of access and which in general are also associated with tertiary activities. The differential annual mean growth rates between EAP and EAFP show an increase in the number of women in these occupations. The increase in the number of women in occupations within the managerial category should be underlined.

This tendency, which indicates the acceptance of women's ability to perform traditionally 'masculine' jobs, has also been observed in Argentina and Chile (Kirsch, 1975). These first three categories in Table 19 absorb 52.3 per cent of the intercensal increase, which is 8.3 per cent for EAP. It should also be borne in mind that EAFP, and to a larger extent EAP, show an important redistribution of the labour force.

In a similar way, the relative significance of 'sales workers' is reduced both at the EAFP and, more markedly so, at the EAP level, resulting in an increase in the number of women in this category. By reason of its

TABLE 19(a). EAP and EAFP by area and by occupation, 1963 and 1975: structure (%)

	Montevideo				Interior			
	EAP		EAFP		EAP		EAFP	
	1963	1975	1963	1975	1963	1975	1963	1975
Professional, technical and related workers	7.9	5.9	13.7	16.3	4.0	5.2	13.4	13.9
Administrative, executive and managerial workers	1.9	2.3	0.3	1.3	0.8	0.8	0.2	0.4
Clerical and related workers	19.7	15.7	18.8	17.8	6.9	6.4	8.0	7.4
Sales workers—excluding itinerant workers	10.1	10.7	7.5	8.9	8.4	8.2	8.6	10.2
Farmers, fishermen, hunters, loggers and related workers	2.1	2.1	0.2	0.3	33.7	27.3	3.2	4.7
Miners, quarrymen and related workers	0.0	0.0	0.0	0.0	0.4	0.3	0.0	0.0
Workers in transport and communication occupations	4.0	3.3	0.0	0.1	3.1	2.3	0.1	0.0
Craftsmen, production process workers in spinning, carpentry, etc.	21.9	19.2	19.0	15.7	14.6	15.0	16.9	14.0
Other craftsmen and labourers	7.5	7.8	4.9	5.9	5.2	6.1	2.5	5.1
Manual workers and day labourers—including itinerant workers	5.1	3.7	1.2	0.8	5.6	3.9	0.6	0.4
Domestic employees	16.8	14.4	(22.0) / 30.9	(18.6) / 24.7	14.5	13.2	(29.0) / 44.4	(29.1) / 34.9
Workers in personal services and related workers			(8.9)	(6.1)			(15.4)	(5.8)
Workers not classifiable by occupation	3.0	10.9	3.3	8.3	2.9	11.4	2.0	8.9
TOTAL	100.0	100.0	100.0	100.0	100.0	100.0	100.0	100.0

Source: National Censuses, 1963 (final data), 1975 (preliminary sample).

TABLE 19(b). EAP and EAFP by area and by occupation, 1963 and 1975: annual mean growth rate (%)

	Montevideo		Interior	
	EAP	EAFP	EAP	EAFP
	1963 1975	1963 1975	1963 1975	1963 1975
Professional, technical and related workers	2.36	2.71	3.46	3.30
Administrative, executive and managerial workers	2.12	10.86	0.59	8.62
Clerical and related workers	−1.61	0.76	0.72	2.32
Sales workers—excluding itinerant workers	0.83	2.50	1.10	4.41
Farmers, fishermen, hunters, loggers and related workers	0.09	4.31	−0.48	5.99
Miners, quarrymen and related workers	−5.75	—	0.0	0.0
Workers in transport and communication occupations	−1.40	5.75	−1.32	0.0
Craftsmen, production process workers in spinning, carpentry, etc.	−0.77	−0.42	1.56	1.41
Other craftsmen and labourers	0.64	2.75	2.77	8.44
Manual workers and day labourers—including itinerant workers	−2.38	−2.78	−1.73	−1.57
Domestic employees	−0.22	−0.22	2.84	3.01
Workers in personal services and related workers	−1.57	−1.95	−1.66	−5.14
Workers not classifiable by occupation	9.97	8.48	11.01	12.59

Source: National Censuses, 1963 (final data), 1975 (preliminary sample).

TABLE 19(c). EAP and EAFP by area and by occupation, 1963 and 1975: distribution of growth (%)

	Montevideo		Interior	
	EAP (1963 1975)	EAFP (1963 1975)	EAP (1963 1975)	EAFP (1963 1975)
Professional, technical and related workers	61.3	33.3	12.1	15.0
Administrative, executive and managerial workers	13.1	7.7	0.4	1.0
Clerical and related workers	−82.7	11.3	3.6	5.9
Sales workers—excluding itinerant workers	25.1	16.7	6.8	14.0
Farmers, fishermen, hunters, loggers and related workers	0.5	1.0	−10.9	8.1
Miners, quarrymen and related workers	−0.5	—	—	—
Workers in transport and communication occupations	−14.7	0.5	−2.6	
Craftsmen, production process workers in spinning, carpentry, etc.	−46.1	−5.9	17.4	7.1
Other craftsmen and labourers	14.1	12.3	11.9	11.3
Manual workers and day labourers—including itinerant workers	−30.4	−2.3	−6.1	−0.2
Domestic employees	−4.2	−3.6	13.7	19.1
Workers in personal services and related workers	−40.8	−11.7	−8.3	−16.7
Workers not classified by occupation	205.2	41.0	62.3	25.4
TOTAL	100.0	100.0	100.0	100.0

Source: National Censuses, 1963 (final data), 1975 (preliminary sample).

59

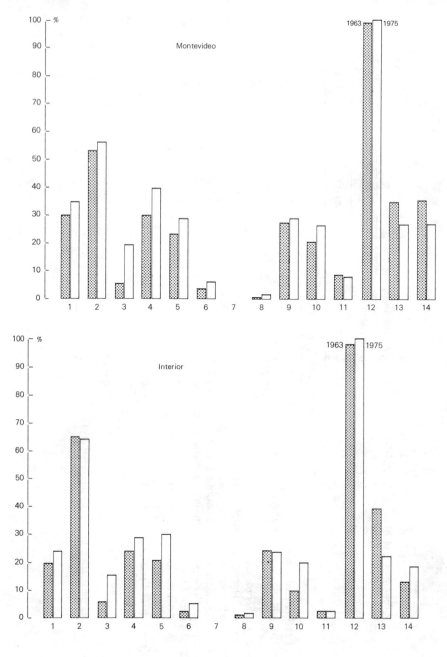

FIG. 7. Proportion of women in the EAP by occupation: 1963 and 1975 (after National Censuses, 1963 (definitive data), 1975 (preliminary sample), as in Appendix Table 4).

1 Total
2 Professional, technical and related workers
3 Administrative, executive and managerial workers
4 Clerical and related workers
5 Sales workers—excluding itinerant workers
6 Farmers, fishermen, hunters, loggers and related workers
7 Miners, quarrymen and related workers
8 Workers in transport and communication occupations
9 Craftsmen, production process workers in spinning, carpentry, etc.
10 Other craftsmen and labourers
11 Manual workers and day labourers—including itinerant workers
12 Domestic employees
13 Workers in personal services and related workers
14 Workers not classifiable by occupation

heterogeneity, it is not useful to include this category in those mentioned before. However, since it explicitly excludes itinerant vendors, it seems reasonable to maintain that these may also be considered to be, in a wider sense, occupations of the middle sectors.

The category of 'domestic employee' offers few difficulties for analysis because of its easy codification and it is also a good indicator of the way in which women are incorporated into the labour market. During the intercensal period not only does it lose in relative significance, falling from 22 per cent of the total for 1963 to 18.6 per cent in 1975, but also in absolute significance, as shown by the average annual growth rates. This decreasing tendency of 'domestic service' has also been observed in Chile (Kirsch, 1975).

For the interior, separate information by area and by sex is not available. The analysis is therefore based on the total for the interior. Given the high percentage (basically masculine) of occupations in the primary sector at the level of EAP, emphasis is placed on the tendencies and not on the comparison of the relative weights between EAP and EAFP.

In this respect and contrary to Montevideo, the tendencies of EAFP and EAP are similar for the three first categories together. However, from the point of view of the annual mean growth rates, an increase in the number of women may be observed when compared with the number of men in the categories of managers, administrators and clerical workers.

With regard to 'professionals, technicians and related workers' the high percentage of women should be noted. Nevertheless, the distribution of the subcategories by sex is significant. Of the total of males in the category, 44 per cent are professionals, while among females the figure is only 4 per cent. Taking into account those occupations related to health and education—traditionally feminine ones, since they constitute a prolongation of their 'natural functions'—it may be observed that 30 per cent of the men are found in these occupations, as compared with 80 per cent of the women's total.[1] As regards the distribution according to sex in each subcategory, 87 per cent of the professionals are males, who represent only 17 per cent of the remaining subcategory.

In the capital the pattern is similar, although less marked because of greater occupational diversification. In this respect, 58 per cent of the men and 13 per cent of the women are professionals, while in the subgroup of teachers, nurses, etc., 16 per cent are men and 63 per cent are women. The internal distribution by sex shows that 79 per cent of the

1. The subcategory includes: nurses (male and female) and midwives; professors and teachers.

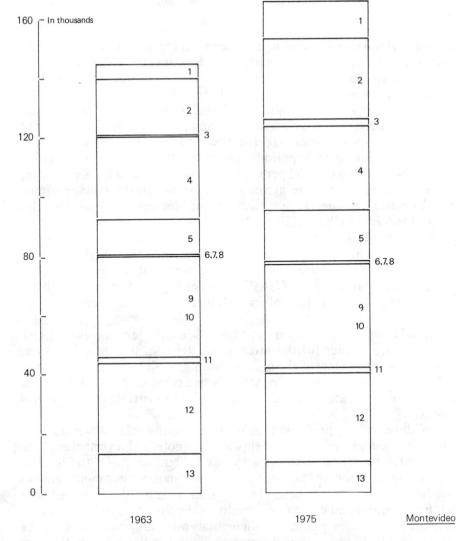

FIG. 8(a). Montevideo: EAFP by occupations, 1963 and 1975 (after National Censuses, 1963 (definitive data), 1975 (preliminary sample), as in Appendix Table 5).

1 Workers not classifiable by occupation
2 Professional, technical and related workers
3 Administrative, executive and managerial workers
4 Clerical and related workers
5 Sales workers—excluding itinerant workers
6 Farmers, fishermen, hunters, loggers and related workers
7 Miners, quarrymen and related workers
8 Workers in transport and communication occupations
9 Craftsmen, production process workers in spinning, carpentry, etc.
10 Other craftsmen and labourers
11 Manual workers and day labourers—including itinerant workers
12 Domestic employees
13 Workers in personal services and related workers

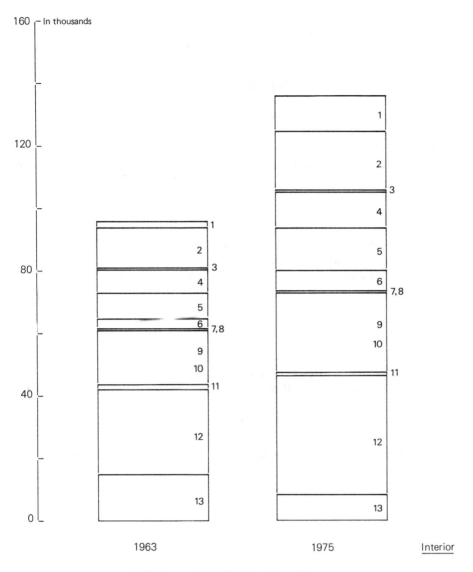

160 ⌐ In thousands

120

80

40

0

1963

1975

Interior

1 Workers not classifiable by occupation
2 Professional, technical and related workers
3 Administrative, executive and managerial workers
4 Clerical and related workers
5 Sales workers—excluding itinerant workers
6 Farmers, fishermen, hunters, loggers and related workers
7 Miners, quarrymen and related workers
8 Workers in transport and communication occupations
9 Craftsmen, production process workers in spinning,
  carpentry, etc.
10 Other craftsmen and labourers
11 Manual workers and day labourers—including itinerant
  workers
12 Domestic employees
13 Workers in personal services and related workers

FIG. 8(b). Interior: EAFP by occupations, 1963 and 1975 (after National Censuses, 1963 (definitive data), 1975 (preliminary sample), as in Appendix Table 5).

63

professionals are males, their figure being 18 per cent in the other category.

The differences in the relative weight between Montevideo and the interior of professional females may stem from the fact that in order to pursue university studies the women who live in the interior have to move to Montevideo. The 'over-protected dependency' of the young women is also likely to be influential in this matter, making the move to Montevideo more difficult.

These aspects deserve special attention, since they constitute a good indicator of women's place in society. The men are concentrated in positions of greater hierarchical importance and greater social value. Women are concentrated, most clearly, in occupations which, even at the lowest point of the scale, are also of an inferior kind. In this sense the Uruguayan case is no exception to the general rule.

Domestic service is an occupation which is important for the analysis of the EAFP. It should be noted that while it maintains its relative weight throughout the intercensal period in the interior, as shown by the annual mean growth rate, it increases considerably in absolute figures, absorbing 29 per cent of the increment in the total EAFP.

From the above, it follows that whereas there is a considerable percentage of women in middle-level occupations, there is also an important percentage in the clearly popular occupations. The different relative weights of both the highest and lowest-scale occupations in Montevideo and the interior, reveal what might be called two 'particular' labour markets.

5 Conclusions and policy implications

Women's participation in the labour market has increased remarkably during the course of the period under study and this increase is striking even in comparison with the figures for a richer and more modern state such as Argentina. The relative total participation should be interpreted bearing in mind the very small weight in the real participation of rural women. The significance of these transformations undoubtedly accentuates a process which has been taking place since the beginning of this century and has led to the social visibility of the economic role of women and, more generally, of their importance in the activities of society and under circumstances which are different from the traditional ones of home and family.

The general features of the forms which this extended participation takes have been described. It is perhaps more difficult to explain the reasons. In the most general terms possible it may be said this process is, in its last instance, determined by the crisis of a development style. It is not the outcome of a continuation of the economic progress and social modernization Uruguay underwent during the first half of this century but, rather of exactly the opposite. As far as women's participation is concerned, this reversal of the process accelerated the tendency for which the first stage of expansion had provided the stimulus. It would serve no useful purpose here to give a precise characterization of this style of development, in itself a concept of vague limits. Suffice it to remember that the following were important. First, there was the economic growth based on the agro-export expansion until the 1930s and on the substitutive industrialization of imports. Second, there was rapid progress in social development. The outstanding feature of the latter is perhaps the expansion in education, which by the extension of its influence and its early characteristics is matchless in the Latin American context, except for neighbouring Argentina. In contrast with Argentina, however, education developed in a more secular and liberal society in which powerful persons and dominant élites had generally less relative and absolute significance. Third, political participation was in permanent expansion as the democratic characteristics of the political process developed.

The reason or reasons why this style of development reached a crisis will not be discussed. However, taking this fact as a starting point, at least four significant points may be made to explain the transformation of women's participation in the labour market.

First, social modernization is responsible for the presence and eventual availability of large contingents of relatively highly educated females, already socialized in an ideology in which women's remunerated work is totally legitimate—if not desirable.

Second, the magnitude of the crisis, its impact on real salary and on family income—within the context of an open society with great penetration of mass media and through it of consumption models characteristic of developed contexts—results in the relative deprivation of large social sectors where women, either to earn or at least not to lose, find themselves strongly stimulated to enter the labour market.

Third, there is little doubt that this very relative deprivation is the fundamental moving power behind international migration without precedent in this country, and because this migration is in its majority masculine, qualified and young, it frees occupational positions for those qualified women who are now also motivated.

Fourth, the lack of rural dynamics in this style of development has always generated the expulsion of population generally and of women in particular. There is also the influence of the forms of agricultural exploitation since the great majority in the rural areas are small family landowners and tenants. For this reason they present a much more balanced population in breakdown by sex and the crisis has a double impact on women. As in the urban case, the deterioration of the family income stimulates the search for palliatives but, also, by eliminating the possibility of paid labour, increases the load of family work including that for women.

The crisis in the development style appears to be the fundamental determinant in the expansion in women's economic participation, *both* directly, through the pressure on the family income, *as well as* indirectly, through the mediation of the migratory processes and particularly of international migration. Thus, urban and urban–metropolitan migrations are in their majority feminine while international migration—to a large extent metropolitan–international—concerns young men.

For that reason, the increase of female participation in Montevideo may be described as a process of mobility by replacement, by which women—of high average formal education—proceed to occupy typically middle-sector positions, mainly in the services sector. This expansion in the Montevidean female economic participation contributes in turn towards generating new occupations precisely because it is the very strength of the crisis which hits the metropolitan middle strata—jointly with other processes—that contributes to limiting the significance of domestic service, a traditional occupational source for women.

In the urban interior more 'balanced' processes develop than in Montevideo: the incorporation of women into the labour market is just as pronounced and the characteristic of participation in the middle sectors is increased. This is accompanied, however, by an increase in the participation in popular sectors, where the most outstanding feature is the maintenance of the relative weight of domestic service.

In the rural interior, the worsening of the situation of the small landowners and rural tenants leads to decreases in paid labour and corresponding increases in family work. Women thus take on tasks in addition to those they traditionally fulfil. The economic visibility of these tasks indicates that women are replacing a part of the paid labour force.

Undoubtedly there are differences between the rural woman who increases her load of daily chores by working in the fields or weaving and knitting for others, and the woman of the urban middle sectors who, to compensate for the deterioration in the family income, turns to paid work. Both situations are, however, the results of a common process and both produce a common result: the growing visibility of the economic importance of women's work.

Some policy suggestions

The insertion of women into the Uruguayan labour market was already high towards 1963 compared with the situation in the large majority of the countries of the region, and this feature became even more acute by 1975. Whereas this characteristic reflects structural factors, the increment during the intercensal period is in all likelihood caused by circumstantial reasons.

We may take it for granted that women's participation in the labour market is a desirable phenomenon for the female condition in general. It implies among other things the social recognition of the importance of their contribution to society. However, in order to outline some policies with reference to women's situation in the labour market it is necessary to take into account some questions which are raised by the analysis.

Will the same levels of activity be maintained if the economic recession finds a positive solution, and especially if there is an improvement in income levels? Will not the slowing-up process of international migration—or its disappearance in socially important terms—signify a backward step for women, in so far as opportunities for work are concerned, revealing what has been noted in other contexts, that is, their characteristic as a secondary labour force?

Since there should be a favourable attitude towards remunerative work by women, the policies recommended should tend to support their participation in order to maintain the levels achieved and if possible to raise them, beyond the influence of the socio-economic conditions which gave rise to it.

Within this general perspective, it is possible to emphasize two recommendations which are considered of basic importance for the future: (a) the development of an infrastructure which will provide concrete support for women's incorporation into the labour market and, (b) measures to improve their specialization and competitivity for access to the labour market.

The infrastructure

From the point of view of the female condition, the ideal would be that men shared more equally with women the responsibility for all the work that making a home implies. Since this proposal appears for the moment unrealistic, a first aspect to take into account is the development of an infrastructure which would help women to leave home with no detriment to family life. There must be a group of institutionally organized services which will permit women to withdraw from their traditional tasks, and which will provide adequate conditions for their participation in the labour market.

One of the greatest obstacles to women's participation in the labour market is constituted by the fact that this departure signifies dramatic changes in the smooth running of home life. In this sense, if women realize that their responsibilities are adequately taken on by others, they are more inclined to participate.

Among the multiple services which it would be advisable to provide, is that of children's nurseries. In Uruguay there is a lack of free or relatively inexpensive services and in many cases not only are the existing ones very expensive in economic terms but they do not offer the desired quality, either in trained personnel or adequate premises. In fact, there has been a proliferation of private nurseries, the fundamental objective of which is not that of service to the community but of profit. They are not therefore useful to those more urgently in need of paid work. These women are obliged to leave their small children alone, or in charge of another child who though somewhat older is not sufficiently so to take on that responsibility.

Measures to improve women's specialization and competitivity for access to the labour market

It is unacceptable that women who have to work should have to do so in tasks for which they have not been specifically trained. This favours their taking on functions related to what is considered their 'natural' ones, for which they receive very low wages: sewing, knitting, housework, cooking, child-care, care of the old and sick, etc. While the final objective should be a substantial change in the distribution of work according to sex, for the time being it does not appear feasible to change the traditional pattern of the prolongation of the 'natural' functions: even the developed countries have not achieved true equality in this aspect. Specialization in no matter what type of work not only qualifies women for better jobs, which are more highly paid, but also predisposes them psychologically to appreciate their own work because of the time spent in training, and in consequence to demand higher pay.

There is a collection of tasks which women carry out very informally and which are sometimes paid but more often not. Here we shall refer in particular to women over 45 years old—a very important group in Uruguay in numerical terms— who are in the prime of life, who have reached the end of the stage of looking after their children, with all that this signifies as far as their free time goes. The possibility of becoming formally incorporated into the labour market is non-existent in socially relevant terms. While this impossibility reflects the negative demand, it is no less a fact that the adult woman does not have a qualification which will permit her to compete in the market. Frequently women of this age turn to the care of the old or of children, in the best of cases as remunerative work but in the majority to help the family. Thus the adult and even old women constitute a rearguard labour force to support the women who work outside the home. If the housewife's situation is a negative one for the female, that of the adult woman who carries out this function in a home other than her own is even more unjust. In general, she participates by working when necessary, being excluded from the remaining activities, especially those of decision-making. The instrumental characteristic of her participation is very explicit.

If what has been said so far is related to the first proposal, specialization for women who have reached advanced adulthood, who are available for formal incorporation into the labour market but who find admission difficult, can be put forward as a specific policy. The proposed organization and institutionalization of services, as well as co-operation to help women to go out to work, might constitute an important source of work for the adult woman. In this way, a set of activities carried out informally would be rationalized, contributing to the elimination of an important source of dependency among a large group of women. A co-ordinated plan of services and human resources within the proposed guidelines would contribute to improving the situation not only of the women who go out to work without having adequate support at home, but also of those who in fact perform a set of tasks for which they are not paid.

Nevertheless, a policy of specialization for women must not exhaust itself in training them to carry out efficiently tasks related to their 'natural' functions, which would reinforce even more their relegation to a particular type of work, with little accepted social value. This initiative should be directed towards those women who are already engaged in a certain type of activity, in order to improve a de facto situation. A general policy of specialization and training should incorporate as its objective a diversification in women's field of work, a task which in reference to the Uruguayan context is reasonably viable, given the high female participation rate in formal education.

These policies are by no means the only ones necessary to improve women's position within the labour market. It is more a matter of focusing on those which are considered feasible, given that there are specific circumstances favourable to women's insertion in the EAP. The complexity of the problem of women's social relegation, in particular the difficulty in encouraging policies to eliminate that relegation, is reduced if women enlarge the scope of their participation in the labour force and do more qualified work. In other words, the constitution of a female labour force, numerous and difficult to find a substitute for, contributes to—or is a necessary condition for—the viability of numerous policies which it would otherwise be difficult to develop successfully.

Appendix

Economic characteristics
of the population

1963

All persons aged 8 years and over were asked about the type of activity they carried out *on the day of the census* (criterion: labour force). Subsequently, the decision was taken to tabulate responses from the population aged 10 years and over. Purely practical reasons recommended this measure. Because the criterion 'labour force' and not 'remunerated worker' was adopted, non-remunerated family workers were included in the active population provided they worked at least 3 hours per day or the equivalent of two 8-hour working days a week (Manual of Census Taker of the IV General Population Census and II of Dwelling).

Branch of activity

Classification of the active population by branch of activity was done according to the Uniform International Industrial Classification of all Economic Activities.

Occupation

Classification of the active population by occupation was done in accordance with the Uniform International Classification of Occupations proposed by IASI in the Program for the census of the Americas—1960 (preliminary sampling of census results—IV General Population Census and II of Dwelling).

1975

All persons aged 12 years and over were questioned about the type of activity they carried out during the week preceding the day of the census.

Because the criterion of 'labour force' and not 'remunerated worker' was adopted, non-remunerated family workers were included under active population provided they worked at least 15 hours per week (Manual of Census Taker of the V General Population Census and III of Dwelling).

Branch of activity

List of codes in the Uniform International Industrial Classification of all Economic Activities.

Occupation

List of codes based on the Occupational Classification (Cota-1970) of the Program for the Census of America—1970.

TABLE 1. Rates of activity by areas and age, both sexes (%)

1963

Age	Total		Montevideo		Urban interior		Rural interior	
	Male	Female	Male	Female	Male	Female	Male	Female
10–14	13.2	13.1	5.0	3.1	17.8	18.6	17.7	3.0
15–19	62.7	26.4	54.6	31.3	59.9	26.3	81.6	13.8
20–24	90.8	38.3	87.3	48.1	92.1	35.1	96.2	15.0
25–34	97.0	34.5	96.6	42.8	97.4	31.1	97.6	13.4
35–44	96.7	30.0	96.7	35.7	96.6	29.0	97.3	11.5
45–54	90.4	24.1	88.0	27.1	90.6	24.6	95.6	11.8
55–64	63.8	12.6	54.9	12.8	64.3	13.1	84.7	9.8
65 and over	21.1	3.3	17.8	3.7	16.8	2.5	38.9	3.6

1975

Age	Total		Montevideo		Urban interior		Rural interior	
	Male	Female	Male	Female	Male	Female	Male	Female
12–14	10.8	4.3	3.6	1.4	5.5	3.3	16.3	5.4
15–19	57.0	24.5	48.5	25.9	54.8	23.9	80.7	21.4
20–24	88.9	40.9	83.7	49.1	91.8	36.4	95.8	24.8
25–34	96.3	40.7	95.4	49.9	96.9	36.4	97.2	20.9
35–44	96.8	39.0	96.6	45.5	96.6	37.0	97.8	19.7
45–54	92.4	32.3	92.0	36.0	91.3	31.6	95.1	16.4
55–64	70.0	16.7	65.4	18.4	69.2	15.7	84.1	11.5
65 and over	20.9	3.6	18.4	3.8	17.6	3.1	36.5	4.5

Source: National Censuses, 1963 (definitive data), 1975 (preliminary sample).

TABLE 2. Rates of female activity by marital status and age 1963 and 1975 (%)

Age	1963		
	Marital status		
	Single women	Widows, divorced and separated women	Married women
15–19	31.2	56.1	12.4
20–24	56.9	64.4	20.0
25–34	67.2	70.5	24.1
35–44	63.0	58.9	22.8
45–54	48.0	34.4	18.2
55–64	25.9	13.2	8.9
65 and over	5.5	1.8	2.2

Age	1975		
	Marital status		
	Single women	Widows, divorced and separated women	Married women
15–19	25.8	50.0	14.1
20–24	55.4	55.6	24.8
25–34	71.2	69.8	30.7
35–44	69.4	70.0	31.0
45–54	55.7	49.6	25.1
55–64	29.7	19.5	12.6
65 and over	7.4	2.6	3.4

Source: National Censuses, 1963 (definitive data), 1975 (preliminary sample).

TABLE 3. Refined rates of activity by sex and area (%) (excluding those looking for work for the first time)

	1963		1975	
	Male	Female	Male	Female
Total of the country[1]	81.2	26.1	78.1	29.4
Montevideo	77.3	30.0	75.0	32.6
Total of the interior	81.8	20.5	79.9	25.0
Urban interior	78.1	24.0	76.7	27.0
Rural interior	88.2	11.7	86.9	17.6

1. Including those looking for work for the first time. Population of age 15 years and over.
Source: National Censuses, 1963 (definitive data), 1975 (preliminary sample).

TABLE 4. Proportion of EAFP in the EAP by occupation (%) 1963 and 1975

	Montevideo		Interior	
	1963	1975	1963	1975
Professional, technical and related workers	53.7	56.0	64.2	62.9
Administrative, executive and managerial workers	5.6	19.3	4.8	13.3
Clerical and related workers	29.4	38.7	22.4	27.0
Sales workers—excluding itinerant workers	23.0	28.0	19.8	29.4
Farmers, fishermen, hunters, loggers and related workers	3.0	5.0	1.8	4.0
Miners, quarrymen and related workers	0.0	0.0	0.0	0.0
Workers in transport and communication occupations	0.5	1.3	0.6	0.8
Craftsmen, production process workers in spinning, carpentry, etc.	26.7	27.8	22.3	21.9
Other craftsmen and labourers	20.1	25.8	9.3	19.6
Manual workers and day labourers—including itinerant workers	7.5	7.2	2.2	2.2
Domestic employees	98.8	99.0	96.5	98.5
Workers in personal services and related workers	32.0	26.2	38.5	21.6
Workers not classifiable by occupation	32.9	25.8	12.9	18.3

Source: National Censuses, 1963 (definitive data), 1975 (preliminary sample), as Table 3.

TABLE 5. EAFP by occupation (in thousands) 1963 and 1975

	Montevideo		Interior	
	1963	1975	1963	1975
Professional, technical and related workers	19.8	27.2	19.9	19.0
Administrative, executive and managerial workers	0.5	2.2	0.2	0.6
Clerical and related workers	27.2	29.7	7.7	10.1
Sales workers—excluding itinerant workers	10.9	14.6	8.3	14.0
Farmers, fishermen, hunters, loggers and related workers	0.3	0.5	3.1	6.4
Miners, quarrymen and related workers	0.1	0.2	0.1	0.1
Workers in transport and communication occupations	0.1	0.2	0.1	0.1
Craftsmen, production process workers in spinning, carpentry, etc.	34.6	36.0	18.7	26.2
Other craftsmen and labourers	34.6	36.0	18.7	26.2
Manual workers and day labourers—including itinerant workers	1.8	1.3	0.6	0.5
Domestic employees	31.8	31.0	27.9	39.7
Workers in personal services and related workers	12.8	10.2	14.8	8.0
Workers not classifiable by occupation	4.7	13.8	1.9	12.2

Source: National Censuses, 1963 (definitive data), 1975 (preliminary sample), as Table 3.

TABLE 6. Population of 15 years age and over according to educational levels

	1963		1975	
	Male	Female	Male	Female
Illiterates	11.4	11.9	7.7	8.7
Some primary	44.6	41.8	34.9	31.1
Primary completed	23.3	27.2	27.7	30.3
Secondary	11.8	11.9	13.1	14.4
Pre-university, some university, teacher training	3.6	5.0	7.4	10.6
University	1.8	0.5	1.7	1.0
Middle-level technical	3.6	1.8	7.4	4.1
TOTAL	100.0	100.0	100.0	100.0

Source: National Censuses, 1963 (definitive data), 1975 (preliminary sample), as Table 3.

References

ALBERTS, J. 1977. *Migración hacia áreas metropolitanas de América Latina*. Santiago de Chile, CELADE.

BARRAN, J. P.; NAHUM, B. 1979. *El Uruguay del Novecientos*. Montevideo, Ediciones de la Banda Oriental.

CARDONA, R.; SIMMONS, A. 1978. *Destino la metrópoli: Un modelo general de las migraciones internas en América Latina*. Bogotá, CCRP.

COCCHI, A.; KLACZKO, J.; RIAL, J. 1977. Una red urbana ordenadora de un espacio vacío: el caso uruguayo. *Cuadernos CIESU*, Vol. 21 (Montevideo).

DE RIZ, L. 1975. El problema de la condición femenina en América Latina. In: CEPAL, *Mujeres en América Latina*. Mexico City, Fondo de Cultura Económica.

DIRECCIÓN GENERAL DE ESTADÍSTICA Y CENSOS 1976. *Encuesta de emigración internacional*. Montevideo.

——. 1979. *Migración internacional 1963-1975*. Montevideo.

ELIZAGA, J. C. 1970. *Migraciones a las áreas metropolitanas de América Latina*. Santiago de Chile, CELADE.

ELTON, C. 1978. *Migración femenina en América Latina: Factores determinantes*. Santiago de Chile, CELADE.

FILGUEIRA, C. 1970. Imbalance y movilidad en la estructura social. *Cuadernos de Ciencias Sociales* (Instituto de Ciencias Sociales, Montevideo) Vol. 3.

FORTUNA, J. C. 1980. La acumulación dependiente y el mercado de fuerza de trabajo en Uruguay. FLACSO, Mexico (M.A. Thesis).

FOUCHER, M. 1977. Argentine: les migrations des travailleurs des pays limitrophes. *Tiers Monde*, Vol. XVIII, No. 69.

GONZALEZ, L. E. 1976. La transformación del sistema político uruguayo. (M.A. Thesis Fundación Bariloche.)

GURR, T. R. 1970. *El porqué de las rebeliones*. Mexico City, Editores Asociados.

HUTCHINSON, B. 1963. The Migrant Population of Urban Brazil. *América Latina* (Río de Janeiro), Vol. 6, No. 2.

INSTITUTO DE ECONOMÍA. 1969. *El proceso económico del Uruguay*. Montevideo, Universidad de la República.

KIRSCH, H. 1975. La participación de la mujer en los mercados laborales latinoamericanos. In: CEPAL, *Mujeres en América Latina*. Mexico City, Fondo de Cultura Económica.

LEE, E. 1965. A Theory of Migration. In: J. A. Jackson (ed.), *Migrations*. Cambridge, Cambridge University Press.

MACADAR, L.; REIG, N.; SANTÍAS, E. 1971. Una economía Latinoamericana. In: L. Benvenuto et al., *Uruguay hoy*. Buenos Aires, Siglo XXI.

McGREEVEY, W. P. 1968. Causas de la migración interna en Colombia. In: CEDE, *Empleo y desarrollo en Bogotá*. Bogotá, Universidad de los Andes.

MARSHALL, A. 1978. *El mercado de trabajo en el capitalismo periférico: el caso de Argentina*. Santiago de Chile, CLACSO-PISPAL.

NAHUM, B. 1975. *La época batllista (1905–1929)*. Montevideo, Ediciones de la Banda Oriental.

NIEDWOROK, N. 1979*a*. Elementos básicos para el estudio de las migraciones internas en el Uruguay. Montevideo, CIESU. (Mimeo).

——. 1979*b*. El crecimiento de la población y sus componentes, Uruguay 1963–1975. Montevideo, CIESU. (Mimeo).

NIEDWOROK, N.; PRATES, S. 1979. Estructura organizativa de la producción rural y dinámica poblacional del sector rural. Montevideo, CIESU. (Mimeo).

PANTELIDES, E. 1976. *Estudio de la población femenina económicamente activa en América Latina, 1950–1970*. Santiago de Chile, CELADE.

PRATES, S. 1976. Ganadería extensiva y población: las condiciones de emergencia de un tipo organizativo de la producción rural. *Cuadernos CIESU* (Montevideo), Vol. 17.

PRATES, S.; TAGLIORETTI, G. 1980. La participación de la mujer en el mercado de trabajo uruguayo: características básicas y evolución reciente. *Cuadernos CIESU* (Montevideo), Vol. 27.

QUIJANO, M. 1972. El batllismo: su política fiscal y la burguesía agraria entre 1900–1930. *Cuadernos de Ciencias Sociales* (Instituto de Ciencias Sociales) (Montevideo), Vol. 2.

RECCHINI DE LATTES, Z. 1980. La participación económica femenina en la Argentina desde la segunda postguerra hasta 1970. *Cuadernos CENEP* (Buenos Aires), Vol. 11.

RIAL, J. 1980. El Estado y la mujer: Legislación tendiente a su protección y a la obtención de la igualdad de los sexos. Montevideo, CIESU. (Mimeo).

THURROW, L. 1972. Education and Economic Equality. *The Public Interest* (New York), Vol. 28.